Protestant-Catholic Marriage

PROTESTANT-CATHOLIC MARRIAGE

C. Stanley
Lowell

BROADMAN
PRESS

Nashville, Tennessee

This book is for Hadley and Cadance
whose blessed interruptions frequently
delayed its production

© 1962 • BROADMAN PRESS
Nashville, Tennessee

422-07224

Library of Congress catalog card number: 62-15326
Printed in the United States of America
5.MH626

Preface

A Protestant theologian who was kind enough
to preview these pages expressed his disapproval thus:
"The trouble with your book is that it takes a viewpoint."
In the academic circles of a certain kind of Protestantism
today the crime celébrè is to espouse a point of view. One
is supposed to accumulate facts and present them. But to
take a position in regard to these facts is regarded as gauche.
Scholars, it is contended, are persons who never "take
sides." When they do so they are no longer scholars. Hence,
a scholarly book is one that does not take a viewpoint.

This book on *Protestant-Catholic Marriage* rejects the
point of view that scholarship cannot take a point of view.
The point of view taken in these pages does not preclude
a presentation of facts. The facts are here. For example,
the Protestant who wants to know the kind of commitments
which will be demanded of him as the price of a marriage
before a Roman Catholic priest can find them here. He can
find the very forms he will be required to sign.

The person interested in Roman Catholic legislation on
the subject of mixed marriage can find reproduced here
the relevant sections of canon laws. These laws are
officially printed in Latin only, but the English translation
used here is approved by the Church and is quite adequate.

Someone who wants to know what major Protestant groups have had to say on the subject of birth control can find here a number of such pronouncements. I believe that this book will have value as a ready source of facts.

I have always felt, however, that scholarship which refuses to draw conclusions from facts is merely irresponsible. In these pages I have not hesitated to draw conclusions. They are set forth in all candor. Roman Catholic leaders will take issue with these conclusions. They must necessarily do so because the conclusions stated here deny the very basis on which they have traditionally drawn their own conclusions in this field. My conclusions will be challenged, again, by Protestants who coddle themselves with a tolerance so broad and vacuous that it will accept anything. But Protestants unashamed, Protestants interested in their own survival will, I believe, find this exploration of the problem of interfaith marriage helpful and constructive.

I, for one, believe that the time has come to stop this mawkish cry of "bigot" whenever positive Protestant convictions are stated. I have nothing against any person or any group. I am a Protestant whose forebears for generations have been Protestants. I am an American dedicated to the American traditions of justice and fair play. I believe in democracy and freedom. I believe that these ideals are relevant even to interfaith marriage. In these pages I have not hesitated to say so.

C. STANLEY LOWELL

Contents

Yes, It's a Problem

1

If you are a Protestant and marry a Roman Catholic the chances that your marriage will break up are about three times as great as if you married a Protestant. Father Lucius P. Cervantes, S.J., director of sociology at Regis College, Denver, has placed the figure at four times rather than three.[1] Studies made in Michigan, Maryland, and Washington, D.C., covering twenty-five thousand families, found that the divorce rate in Protestant-Catholic marriages approached the figure cited above—nearly three times higher than in marriages where both parties are of the same faith.[2]

Protestant and Roman Catholic clergymen are in complete agreement on the undesirability of interfaith marriages. Virtually every principal denomination has taken a strong stand against them. The General Conference of the Methodist Church, meeting in Minneapolis, Minnesota, in April, 1956, made this pronouncement: "It is strongly urged that each young person consider carefully before becoming engaged to anyone who does not have a similar religious background. It is important that Protestant youth discuss this problem with their ministers before it is too late. Ministers are urged to discuss with both youth and parents the likelihood of failure in mixed marriages."

1

The Lutheran Church, Missouri Synod, took a somewhat sharper position when it warned its members against mixed marriages which "condemn unborn children to the soul-destroying religion of the antichrist"—an apparent reference to one of the commitments in the antenuptial agreement. The annual Synod of the Augustana Evangelical Lutheran Church, meeting in June, 1956, sounded a warning against its members' marrying Roman Catholics. It noted that such unions "often result in marital unhappiness and disruption of normal home life for the children affected," that they tend to "create situations having far-reaching psychological, social, economic, and spiritual consequences," and that these "very often involve the danger of the denial of faith." The General Convention of the Protestant Episcopal Church in 1949 adopted its own version of a previous Lambeth declaration. It "earnestly warns members of our Church against contracting marriages with Roman Catholics under conditions imposed by modern Roman Catholic Canon Law."

There is a popular notion that Roman Catholic priests are favorable to mixed marriages as a means of converting Protestants. It is probably false. All of this church's literature on the subject is solidly oriented against its members' marrying Protestants. The Roman Church has, in fact, a sweeping prohibition against all such marriages (Canon 1060). Since it has proved impossible to maintain such a rule in practice, this church grants what it calls a "dispensation" for a mixed marriage on terms which provide that its denominational interests will be fully protected.

Church Rigidity Fails

With all their vaunted rigidity on the subject, many Roman Catholic experts acknowledge that their policy on mixed marriage has been a failure. That is to say, they lose more than they gain through such marriages. In a study of 305 Catholic-Protestant marriages conducted by Professor Judson Landis, 113 of the parties changed religion. Fifty-six Protestants became Catholics and fifty-seven Catholics became Protestants.[3] Noting that one-third of all Catholics marry outside their faith, Father Cervantes said that of every ten who do so "four are lost immediately . . . since their marriage is outside of the Church and hence invalid. Of the six out of the ten remaining in the faith . . . two more are ultimately lost because their interest and conformity gradually evanesce."[4]

In spite of the apparently airtight commitments regarding the children which Roman Catholic clerics demand in mixed marriages, figures indicate that here, too, they fail as often as they succeed. Dr. John J. Kane, the Notre Dame sociologist, reports that in mixed marriages where neither party changed his religion 50 per cent reared the children as Protestants, 45 per cent as Catholics and 5 per cent without any religion.[5] He remarks: "Chances are a little better than even that your children will not be reared as Catholics." The Bishops' Committee of the Roman Catholic Church reported that the promises regarding the Catholic rearing of children were not kept in 30 per cent of the valid mixed marriages.[6] But *Ave Maria,* nationally known Catholic weekly, estimates that the promises are kept in only 30 per cent of the cases.[7] A Y.M.C.A. survey of men between the ages of sixteen and thirty-five in representative urban and rural districts showed that where both parents were Roman Catholic, 92 per cent of their sons practiced this faith; where both were Protestant, 68 per cent were practicing Protestants; where one was Catholic and the other Protestant, only 34 per cent of their sons practiced either faith.[8]

The theologian Father Francis J. Connell laments "the terrible inroads on the Catholic faith caused by mixed marriages."[9] Father Raymond J. Neufeld says bitterly: "Look at this miserable figure; 60 per cent of Catholics marrying non-Catholics defect from the faith.[10] So far as the clergy is concerned, Protestant and Roman Catholic alike, mixed marriage is a venture which does nobody any good. Protestants feel that they lose as a result of the promises exacted by the Roman Church in its antenuptial agreement. Catholics feel that the promises are indifferently kept or not kept at all in many instances, and that their church loses. All agree that the added strains which the religious differences impose on the marriage make it far more prone to failure.

Yet, despite the warnings of the clergy and the sound advice of marriage counselors, there is an astonishingly large number of Protestant-Catholic marriages and the number is increasing. A resolution adopted by the National Catholic Family Life Convention acknowledges that from one-fourth to one-third of all marriages involving Roman Catholics are interfaith unions.[11] A majority of these are no doubt "unthinking marriages" in which young people meet, become emotionally attracted, and proceed to get married. But a considerable number, too, are cases in which, after apparent consideration and extensive counseling with both Protestant and Roman Catholic clergy, the step is taken.

Mixed Marriages Persist

How many Protestant-Catholic marriages are there? *The Official Roman Catholic Directory of 1960* lists 81,302 mixed marriages of all types, the overwhelming majority being Protestant-Catholic. This compares with 79,839 listed in the 1954 *Directory*. The United States Census Bureau, on the basis of a sampling survey, has estimated that one Protestant in twelve who is married has a Catholic spouse and that one Catholic in five has a Protestant spouse. This involves an estimated total of 4,510,000 persons who are partners in mixed marriage.

The breakdown of mixed marriage statistics by individual dioceses can be startling. Msgr. Louis F. Miltenberger, a Washington, D.C. pastor, informed a sociological convention that there are as many valid mixed marriages in that city as purely Catholic marriages.[12] The actual figures in the 1960 *Directory* are *1,448* Catholic and *1,442* mixed. But statistics of this kind, impressive as they are, do not give the full picture. Roman Catholic statistics, as a rule, deal only with mixed marriages that have been performed by a priest. The number of such marriages performed by clergy of other denominations and civil officials is probably as great. A survey conducted by the United Lutheran Church indicated that in 1958 there were 3,343 marriages between its members and Roman Catholics and that two-thirds of these were performed by Lutheran pastors.[13] Father John L. Thomas in his study, previously alluded to, reports that in 132 representative parishes 39.6 per cent of the mixed marriages were not performed by priests.[14] The *Ave Maria* admits that the number of "invalid" mixed marriages may be almost as large as the number performed by priests.[15]

The number of mixed marriages, under both Roman Catholic and Protestant auspices, is increasing. Father Thomas shows a steady increase over a period of a decade. Professor Kane predicts an increase to 50 per cent in "valid" mixed marriages alone.[16] The breakdown of Roman Catholic religious ghettos and the increasing inability of religiously segregated parish schools to accommodate the rising numbers of Catholic pupils, are further indicators. Very significantly, too, there seems to be a favorable popular disposition toward such marriages, regardless of the counsels of the clergy. A Gallup poll on the subject indicates that majorities of both Protestant and Roman Catholics would have no serious objection to their child's marrying a member of the other church.[17] The poll showed substantially less objection among Catholics than among Protestants, however. The results:

	Roman Catholics	Protestants
Yes, would object	23 per cent	35 per cent
No, would not object	72 per cent	58 per cent
No opinion	5 per cent	7 per cent

All this indicates that more and more persons are going to be joined in Protestant-Roman Catholic marriages. And it means that the special difficulties which inhere in such unions will be more widely felt. To keep a marriage on an even keel under contemporary pressures is a formidable feat. To take on the mixed marriage pressures is to assume an additional burden which may mean the margin of failure. Yet millions are trying it today and apparently millions more will try it tomorrow. Yes, it's a problem.

The Roman Catholic Position

2

In the Roman Catholic view the primary and dominating purpose of marriage is the procreation and education of children.[1] The strenuous consistency with which the hierarchy supports this view is intelligible only in terms of its devotion to its own institutional values. Its goal in marriage is control—to keep the Catholics Catholic and to make Catholic those who are not. There is a secondary purpose of marriage in the Roman view—the allaying of concupiscence, or the natural sex urge, which is conceived to be the consequence of original sin. But this purpose is definitely secondary and negative.

In Roman Catholic thought marriage is a sacrament of Christian faith. Since priests of this church are held to be the sole authorized custodians of Christian faith, they alone are deemed competent to perform marriages and define their terms. The church recognizes that there are civil effects of marriage, but the marriage bond itself, at least so far as Catholics are concerned, involves a religious rite which is subject to the sole jurisdiction of the Roman Church.

It will be helpful at this point to insert the more important rules of the Roman Catholic Church in regard to marriage as contained in the canon laws.

Canon 1012: Our Lord elevated the very contract of marriage

7

between baptized persons to the dignity of a sacrament. Therefore, it is impossible for a valid contract of marriage to exist without being by that very fact a sacrament.

Canon 1013: The primary end of marriage is the procreation and education of children; its secondary end is mutual help and the allaying of concupiscence. The essential properties of marriage are unity and indissolubility, which acquire a peculiar firmness in Christian marriage by reason of its sacramental character.

Canon 1016: The marriage of baptized persons is governed not only by divine law but also by canon law, without prejudice to the civil power as regards the merely civil effects of such marriage.

Canon 1060: The Church everywhere most severely forbids the contracting of marriage between two baptized persons of whom one is a Catholic whereas the other is a member of an heretical or schismatical sect; and if there is danger of perversion of the Catholic party and the children, the marriage is forbidden by the divine law itself.

Canon 1061: The Church does not dispense from the impediment of mixed religion unless there are just and grave reasons therefor; the non-Catholic party shall have given a guarantee to remove all danger of perversion from the Catholic party and both parties shall have given guarantees to baptize and educate all the children in the Catholic faith alone.

Canon 1062: The Catholic party is obliged to strive prudently for the conversion of the non-Catholic party.

Canon 1063: Even though a dispensation from the impediment of mixed marriage has been obtained from the Church, the parties may not, either before or after the celebration of the marriage before the Church, apply also, either in person or by proxy, to a non-Catholic minister in his religious capacity, in order to express or renew matrimonial consent.

Canon 1070: A marriage contracted by a nonbaptized person with a person who was baptized in the Catholic Church or who has been converted to it from heresy or schism, is null.[2]

It is conceded by the Roman Church that Protestant marriages since 1908, when contracted in sincerity are valid. (The new canon law including this point was proclaimed in 1917). Yet the pope still claims and, on occasion, exercises the right to annul a Protestant marriage. He does so by virtue of his assumed control over all Christian marriages. It is in regard to the marriage of Roman Catholics, however, that the Roman Church makes its strongest claims. Canon 1012 proclaims that for Catholics there can be no valid marriage unless it is performed by a Catholic priest. If a Catholic is married by a Protestant clergyman this is described as "attempted marriage" and not valid. The Catholic partner is adjudged to be living "in low and abominable concubinage." (Pius IX in *Acerbissimum* used the expression *turpem et exitalem concubinatum.*)

The implementation of this view in the local parish is quite as interesting as the canon law itself. The publication of St. Joseph's Roman Catholic Church in Maplewood, New Jersey, carries the following application of the Church rule to its own members: "A Catholic can be married validly and licitly only before his Catholic priest and two Catholic witnesses. No other marriage of a Catholic, even to a non-Catholic, is recognized by the Church for her members. Any other marriage for Catholics is null and void and sinful."

Church Supersedes State

In view of the divine prerogatives which it claims, the Roman Church is quick to assert its own control over marriage as opposed to any claims of the state. This is the reason the church will generally oppose any proposals by the state for procedures to regulate marriage. Even health examinations by the state may be resisted on the ground that such measures impinge on the church's authority in this field.

This exclusive control which the Roman Church professes is underscored by standing rules in a number of United States dioceses to the effect that no attorney of Roman Catholic faith may bring a divorce action in the courts without first clearing it with the bishop. It is argued that only the hierarchy of the Roman Church is competent to decide whether or not a marriage is valid. As Bishop (now Archbishop) John F. Deardon explained the matter to attorneys in the Pittsburgh diocese: "We maintain that an attorney is not competent to judge the existence or nonexistence of the sacred contract of marriage."[3] If the bishop adjudged the marriage to be valid, then the attorney would be barred from bringing a divorce action in a civil court. It is even declared that, because of the Church's complete jurisdiction in this field, the Catholic bishop's judgment on the matter "covers not only cases involving Catholics but Protestants and Jews as well who have contracted valid marriages."[4] The *National Catholic Almanac* (1948) even goes so far as to say that "the state has no right to grant divorces since it has no authority to annul a valid marriage."[5]

The Church's insistence on complete control of marriages involving its members is pointed out by a famous case in Italy in 1958. A young Italian couple, Mauro and Loriana Bellandi, who had been baptized Catholic, were married in a civil ceremony. This is a proper procedure under Italian law. Because, as baptized Roman Catholics, they had presumed to be married by someone other than a Catholic priest, the diocesan bishop, Pietro Fiordelli, issued a pastoral letter calling the young couple "public sinners" and describing the bride as "a harlot and a concubine."[6]

The groom charged the bishop with criminal libel and

an Italian civil court found him guilty and assessed a fine of forty thousand lire. The conviction was reversed in the higher court. The case created a sensation because of its challenge to the Roman Church's monopoly over the marriage of those it declares to be its members. The pope reacted sharply to this challenge from a civil court by excommunicating the judges, the prosecuting attorney (who had actually pleaded for acquittal), and everyone who had had anything to do with the trial.[7] (The bishop himself had refused to appear in court.)

Catholic Law on Mixed Marriage

Canon 1060 forbids mixed marriage for Roman Catholics. But a dispensation permitting a mixed marriage is readily obtainable provided certain conditions are met. The conditions are in the form of concessions by the Protestant partner which are designed to keep the Catholic partner and the children of the union in that church. (See chap. 4.)

Much Roman Catholic teaching emphasizes the permanence of the marriage tie. The popes have reiterated it again and again. For example, Pius XI proclaimed that once assumed, the marriage bond cannot be dissolved. It is highly important for the Protestant to understand, however, that this concern for the permanence of the marriage tie applies only to marriages performed by Roman Catholic priests. If the marriage has been performed by a Protestant minister, a Catholic usually encounters little trouble in getting approval for a civil divorce and remarriage in his church. Books could be filled with such examples. Indeed, there are instances of a second, third, or fourth marriage for Catholics performed by a priest in the Roman Catholic Church.

Some years ago the famous crooner Rudy Vallee married

Eleanor Kathleen Norris, a young girl just out of convent school. They were married in a Roman Catholic Church. Yet it was well-known that the crooner had had a number of previous marriages. Father Richard Ginder, editor of the *Priest*, has provided a detailed explanation of this strange event.[8] The crooner originally married Marian. Then he divorced her and married Peggie. Next he ditched Peggie and married Edith. At this point Marian dropped dead. By a curious coincidence this happened to have been the only one of his previous marriages that had been performed by a priest. Since this was the only marriage that "counted," and since Marian was dead, the crooner was free to marry again in the Church—which he did. What is stressed, quite evidently, is not permanence of marriage so much as the Church's authority and control.

Again there were questions raised by the faithful when the heavyweight boxing champion, Floyd Patterson, who had been married previously, became a convert to the Roman Church and was married to a Catholic girl before a priest. The Catholic expert in these matters explained in the official publication of the Brooklyn diocese that "Floyd Patterson's first marriage was not a valid union. The marriage was performed by a civil official to a girl who was baptized in the Catholic Church."[9] But when Gisele Mac-Kenzie, the TV star, took a similar step without the priest's approval, the same publication bitterly attacked her. It referred to her "marriage" as though it were a shameful relationship and mourned her addition to the "long list of performers who were practicing Catholics until by divorce and/or marriage to a divorced person they put themselves outside the church."[10]

Father Raymond J. Neufeld, a Roman Catholic authority on matters pertaining to marriage, has given a careful answer to the question: "Can a Catholic who was married outside the Faith, then separated and divorced, marry a Catholic in a Catholic ceremony?"[11] He answers: "Yes." Explanation: A Catholic who was married in a ceremony outside the Faith was not really married at all.

It is quite possible that Catholic laymen with an admixture of realism and cynicism take advantage of their church's relative indifference to marriages performed "outside the church." It is evident that they are quite free to jump in and out of marriages so long as they keep clear of the priests. They do run some risk of dying in a "state of sin," but if their health is good they may be willing to chance it. When, in later life, they become penitent and decide to "settle down," they can, at no great inconvenience, be reconciled to the Church and have a nice wedding "for keeps" solemnized by a priest.

Catholics and Divorce

The Roman Catholic Church claims to be "the only great force today which stands in opposition to that frightful evil (divorce)." But is this a valid claim? There is much in the record of this church to indicate that its attitude toward divorce is actually quite casual. It must always be clear that for Catholics the indissolubility of marriage applies only to marriages performed by their own priests. If there is any doubt on this score, consider some further examples.

Tyrone Power, a Roman Catholic, was declared free to marry Linda Christian in Santa Francesa Romana Church in Rome. Power had previously been married to Annabella, also a Catholic, but theirs had been a civil marriage. Hence, Power was free to remarry by merely establishing the facts of his first "nonmarriage." Sloan Simpson, married and divorced, was free to marry again in the Church, this time to then mayor of New York, William O'Dwyer. Her first marriage was not performed by a priest and was, therefore, ruled invalid.

How can the Roman Catholic Church maintain its facade of firm rejection of divorce on the one hand, while it rather freely annuls or dissolves marriages on the other? It does this by setting up its own marriage courts and making its own arrangements in these matters. Actually, the courts are not needed in most instances, since a "divorce" on a variety of causes can be readily and summarily granted by a priest in consultation with his bishop. The expensive recourse to the Church courts is necessary only in more complicated cases. Only a tiny fraction of the total number of cases ever reaches the famed Sacred Roman Rota of whose austerity so much has been made.

The annulment is granted, of course, because some "impediment" invalidated the marriage and, therefore, it is averred that the persons never were really married. One popular ground for invalidation of a marriage is the possibility that either of the parties believed in divorce at the time the ceremony was performed. If either entered the union believing that it might be dissoluble under any circumstances, then it cannot be regarded as a valid and binding marriage.[12] The most prolific of the automatic grounds for nullity is, as we have seen, invalidity of the marriage because it was performed by a Protestant minister or a civil official. Actually, there is hardly a marriage for which a cause for annulment cannot be found. Some of the grounds recognized by the Church are quite trivial and would have no status whatever in an American civil court where an annulment is difficult to obtain. All that is required is some ingenuity in drafting the case and some persistence in carrying it through. If an "appeal" is necessary, the cost can run high. In the long run, however, the matter usually can be worked out, provided one is a good Catholic and plays ball with the Church. The unforgivable offense is to step outside and get a civil divorce without first clearing with the priests.

Sometimes the Church resorts to fantastic gyrations to accommodate a favored son. Thus, after more than forty years of marriage, with children and grandchildren, President Manuel Prado of Peru was able to obtain a solemn pronouncement from the Church that his first marriage had been invalid and that he was free to marry Lima socialite Clorinda Málaga.[18] In its explanation to an incredulous public, Father Ulpiano López, an expert in canon laws, stated that if full mutual consent had not existed in the case of the prior marriage, then that marriage would have been invalid. He offered as an example the case of a man who was compelled to marry under threat of death. Whether he meant that this specifically applied to President Prado the priest did not say. But under some such finding a special panel of clerics was able to approve the annulment of the first marriage and clear the way for the second.

Even when the previous marriage is admittedly valid, the good Catholic desiring to remarry need not altogether despair. A dissolution of such a marriage is still possible. Most popular ground is the so-called "Pauline Privilege" (Canons 1120-1126) which permits a convert to the Roman Church to remarry in that faith provided the original partner refuses to co-operate in the new religion.

Such procedures appear to the onlooker as devious and inconsistent manipulations. Yet there is really one consistent motif: preservation of Roman Catholic control over marriages of its people and the protection of its denominational interests. The point is succinctly made in a statement which

appeared in the "Our Readers Ask" column of the Boston
Pilot. "When a Catholic has entered into a marriage contract, only the Church may pass judgment on his right to
leave his former partner and remarry with another. The
right is determined by the law of God, not by the decrees
of any civil power."[14] (It must be understood, of course,
that the expression "law of God" as used in this quotation
is interpreted by Roman Catholic priests to mean the law
of their church.)

How the Catholic Church Exercises Control

There are various ways in which the Roman Catholic
hierarchy gives emphasis to its control of all matters relating
to marriage and the family. In any negotiations prior to a
Protestant-Catholic marriage priests insist on their right to
have the ceremony in a Roman Church and performed by
one of their own number. This is applied quite as strictly
when the girl is a Protestant as in the opposite case. Their
rigidity at this point is illustrated by an exchange of correspondence between the Most Rev. Thomas J. McDonnell,
Coadjutor Bishop of Wheeling, West Virginia, and Protestant Episcopal Bishop Wilbur C. Campbell of that state.
The correspondence concerned a young couple, a Roman
Catholic boy and a Protestant Episcopal girl, who were to be
married in her church. A Catholic priest had ordered a boy-
cott of the ceremony, even forbidding the boy's mother to
attend, and Bishop Campbell had written to the Catholic
prelate, seeking some easement of the situation. The Roman
Catholic bishop replied:

If he (the groom) enters into this marriage with this young
Episcopalian lady he will be excommunicated from the Church,
his marriage will not be recognized by the Catholic Church, and

in the eyes of the Catholic Church, he will be living in concubinage. In reference to the young man's mother's attitude.
The mother is also not a representative Catholic if she gives
complete approval to such a marriage. The priest was absolutely right in telling her she cannot attend the marriage because it is going to be performed in a non-Roman Catholic
Church. . . . Her being present in the church at the marriage,
although not participating in the service, is also a source of great
scandal to Roman Catholic people. It is for her a matter of
confession.[15]

To most Protestants such a rule seems heartless and cruel.
They are not particularly comforted by the explanation
which is offered by Father John A. O'Brien, nationally
known marriage counselor. He writes:

To sanction the marriage of one of her children before a non-
Catholic minister would mean that the Church was implicitly
recognizing such a denomination, founded by a mere man, to
be of equal validity with the Church established by Jesus Christ.
This the Church could do only at the cost of her intellectual
integrity and of treason to her divine Founder. To place the
various sects founded by mere men such as Martin Luther, an
apostate Augustinian monk, John Calvin, John Knox, John and
Charles Wesley, Mrs. Mary Baker Eddy, and Mrs. Aimee Semple
MacPherson Hutton on the same plane and to clothe them with
the same authority, would be for her to commit the sin of
apostasy.[16]

Roman Catholic priests stress their authority by refusing
to permit Catholic laymen to participate in the wedding
service of another church. Such services are included in the
general ban on attendance and participation in "false worship" (Canon 1258). Yet in the case of weddings and
funerals there can be occasional latitude in the discretion

of the bishop. The law specifies "for reason of civil office or honor, and for a serious reason . . . providing there is no danger of loss of faith or of scandal." The fact that individual requests may be decided by the bishop in his judgment further emphasizes the hierarchy's control in such matters.

A law which admits ambiguous exceptions does, however, lend itself to inconsistent and even capricious enforcement at the local level. Question-and-answer columns in Roman Catholic publications frequently disclose aggrieved queries by those who have been refused permission to participate in a Protestant wedding, yet can point to other cases where the permission was granted. The answering cleric is frequently hard put to explain the patent inconsistencies. One of the less successful efforts is recorded in the *Sign.*[17] An indignant questioner who had been denied permission to participate in an Episcopalian wedding read that Princess Grace of Monaco had been granted permission for a like role. How come? The priest's explanation is that whereas his correspondent had sought permission to be a bridesmaid, Princess Grace had only been a matron of honor and that this accounted for the difference!

Msgr. J. D. Conway stresses the difficulties involved in serving as an attendant at a Protestant wedding: "Attendants give seeming approval to heretical proceedings. In that might lie the principal source of scandal."[18] In case of an invitation to be an attendant at a Protestant wedding, Father Conway's advice is: "If you can possibly get out of it without offense try to do so." If they are not satisfied with this and want to pursue the matter further, they are commended to the parish priest who, in turn, can confer with the bishop. "But remember," Father Conway concludes, "if you ask the pastor or bishop to resolve the doubt for you,

you should be prepared to abide by the decision you receive."

The Church's Strange Persistence

It is difficult for the casual observer to credit the ferocity with which the Roman Catholic hierarchy at times pursues its institutional concern on issues which pertain to marriage and the family. An assistant pastor in a Roman Catholic parish compiled a list of names of Catholics in the area who had been married in a ceremony not performed by a priest and sent them a form letter suggesting that they come in to see about getting their marriage "validated." This could be done either by removal of the original "impediment," or, in more complicated cases, by the *sanatio in radice* (cleansing at the root). In the latter procedure the marriage can be validated and the children born of the union legitimatized even without the consent of one of the partners.

Roman Catholic control of marriage extends even to the grave. America's leading Catholic theologian, Msgr. Francis J. Connell, for many years dean of the School of Sacred Theology of Catholic University, has acknowledged that Roman Catholics who are married by a Protestant clergyman will be punished even in the graveyard. The following is taken verbatim from his statement:

Question: Is it correct to tell Catholics that they will be denied Christian burial in the event that they attempt marriage before a non-Catholic minister?

Answer: Such a statement can be made correctly, as long as the clause is added "unless before death they give some signs of repentance" (Canon 1240, Sec. 1). The reason is that, by such a sinful act, a Catholic becomes a public and manifest sinner, and to such a one Christian burial is denied (Canon 1240, Sec. 1, Note 6).[19]

Bishop Thomas J. Riley was asked if a Protestant husband or wife of a Roman Catholic might be buried beside the other spouse in a Catholic cemetery. (Presumably this would be in case of a "valid" marriage before a priest.) Bishop Riley replied that except in case of special permission, "as a general rule it is not allowable for a non-Catholic to be buried in a cemetery which has been consecrated."[20]

The Diemer case in the courts of New York discloses the lengths to which a parish priest may go in asserting his church's control over marriage and family arrangements.[21] He may even persist to the point of breaking up a happy home. William Diemer was a Presbyterian, his wife a Roman Catholic. They were married in the Presbyterian church following an agreement that any children born of the union would be reared in the Presbyterian faith. The wife subsequently joined the Presbyterian church and attended it for a period. Following the birth of a child the wife was visited by a Roman Catholic priest who informed her that her marriage was not valid in the eyes of that church, that she was "living in sin," and that her child was illegitimate.

The wife became much upset and stated that she wanted to do what she could to rectify the situation with the Roman Catholic Church. The priest advised her that the only way she could continue to live with her husband without sin, should he persist in his refusal to have the marriage "validated" in the Roman Church, would be to refrain from marital relations. She did then deny her husband such relations and continued to do so until he at length separated from her.

Mrs. Diemer testified that Mr. Diemer was a good father, an excellent provider, and a fine husband. With the sole exception of the religious difference between them, she testified that she could ask for no better marriage than she had. All the evidence indicates that the marriage would have been unusually happy and successful had it not been for the clerical interference. Yet the priest was acting in perfect consistency with his church's teaching when he directed the withholding of marital relations until the marriage could be "validated" in the eyes of his church.

Inflexible insistence on control of the child's education is basic to the institutional concern which the Roman Catholic Church invariably exhibits in domestic matters. This insistence extends to every child to which it can establish a claim, even in cases where the claim may be only partial or nominal. A Roman Catholic woman asks a Catholic priest how she can be absolved from her sin. She had borne a child out of wedlock and had immediately given her to her doctor, who was not a Catholic, for adoption. Apparently some years have passed. After discussion with her confessor the woman has come to realize the enormity of her sin in not assuring the child a Catholic upbringing. In her original confessions she failed to mention this matter. Now she has been brought to realize that these confessions were ineffectual and that she is living in a state of sin. The child is happily established in the doctor's home; what can she do?

The priest urges the woman, even at this date, to intervene with the doctor in regard to the child's religious training. "Even now," he writes, "you might be able to prevail, diplomatically, upon the doctor and his wife to give the girl a Catholic upbringing."

The Church in Action

One of the most astonishing instances of persistence in the denominational prerogatives came to full public attention in the case of Hildy Ellis.[22] Hildy's mother, an unwed woman named Marjorie McCoy, who later became Mrs. Marjorie Doherty, entrusted the baby to the care of Mr. and Mrs. Melvin B. Ellis in Massachusetts. Hildy was then only ten days old. The mother claimed she did not know the Ellises were Jewish; the Ellises insisted that she did know this. Hildy spent the next six years in the custody of the Ellises. It was acknowledged generally that the couple made excellent foster parents and that Hildy was happy in their love and care. When the situation came to the attention of the hierarchy, evidently through the confessional, Hildy's natural mother went to court with its backing to wrest Hildy away from the Ellises—not to care for her herself but to place her in a Catholic orphanage where she would receive Catholic training. Mrs. Doherty sought to accomplish this under a 1950 Massachusetts law requiring that adoptive parents must be of the same faith as the child "when practicable."

Archbishop (now Cardinal) Cushing threw the full prestige of the Roman Catholic Church into this battle. He exerted every possible influence on public opinion and on the courts to have Hildy torn from the home where she was loved and cared for by devoted parents and assigned to an institution where she would be reared as a Catholic. To make the child Catholic became the sole concern of the Church to the exclusion of all other concerns in this entire controversy. This is exactly what would have been done by the Massachusetts court had not the Ellises fled its jurisdiction to Florida. There the kindly and humane Governor Leroy Collins refused to extradite them, candidly placing the child's welfare above the Church's demands. Here again, Cardinal Cushing's stand was consistent to the letter with the teaching of his Church which invariably places the denominational interest over all other values.

It is reassuring, incidentally, that some of the most outspoken criticism of the Massachusetts law in connection with the Hildy Ellis case came from Judge Edward Morley of the Gloucester District Court, himself an eminent Roman Catholic layman. He condemned the law under which the Ellises were arraigned as "the offspring of religious bias and prejudice," and called for its replacement with an improved statute under which "the welfare of the child [would] be again made the important element in determining the advisability of allowing a petition for adoption."

Whether the Roman Catholic position is right or wrong, defensible or indefensible, is not the point at the moment. The point is that a Protestant who contemplates marriage with a Roman Catholic contemplates involvement with a church. This involvement will continue to intrude upon the marriage and worry and harass its principals until death or until they yield to its terms. It will, in fact, continue to follow their children after they are gone. If the Protestant partner is willing at the outset, and throughout life, to accept the priest's dictation and control in regard to the wedding and in regard to the rearing of the children, the marriage can continue on an even keel so far as these matters are concerned. If he or she refuses at any point, then there will be pressure, heartache, and the possible breakup of the marriage.

It is true, of course, that the priests of the Roman Catholic Church have no way of enforcing their claims in the United States except through such personal appeals and group pressures as they are able to mount. In the United States, when Catholics defy their priests and make their own decisions in regard to marriage, there is no legal weapon which the Church can employ against them. There are, however, formidable social and spiritual pressures. These are indicated in the article by Msgr. Francis J. Connell. He writes:

When a Catholic contracts an invalid marriage (before a civil magistrate or a non-Catholic clergyman), his friends and especially the members of his family should not accept an invitation to be present. Moreover, social contacts with the pair should be avoided or at least restricted to a minimum when they imply a recognition of the two as husband and wife.[23]

Ostracism of this sort is one of the cruelest forms of torture to which a young couple can be subjected. But there is a still more powerful weapon in the Church's arsenal. This is the excommunication of the Catholic who marries outside his church and the denial of the sacraments to him. The Church teaches that a Catholic who has been married by a Protestant clergyman is living in a state of sin. If he should die in this state, things would go very hard with him indeed. This thought preys on the mind of the recalcitrant one, especially when it is compounded with the tearful anxiety of his parents and friends. Influences of this kind, even when initially impotent, have a way of proving effective in the long run. The Roman Catholic hierarchy has had long experience in conquering independent wills and it never gives up. It is not realistic to underestimate such pressures. These are plain facts which any Protestant who considers a marriage with a Roman Catholic would be foolish not to assess.

The Protestant Position

3

The Protestant concept of marriage is less intransigent, more adaptable, than the Roman Catholic. No Protestant pastor would attempt to extract a signed agreement from the non-Protestant party to a mixed marriage that he or she will bring up the children in the Protestant faith. Protestant clergymen do not rigidly insist on having their own way in the religious situation. They are willing to leave some latitude for give-and-take and for the judgment of the partners themselves.

Catholic priests frequently explain the greater adaptability of the Protestants on the ground of religious indifference. They assert that a Protestant will not insist on having his own way religiously because he considers one religion as good as another. This is not the case. Protestants are quite as convinced of the rightness of their own views as are persons of other faiths. Baptists are Baptists because they believe that Baptists are right. Methodists are Methodists for the same reason. Lutherans are Lutherans because they believe the Lutheran church is nearer the truth than any other. And so with all the rest. Likewise, any Protestant considers his own faith, or that of any other Protestant, superior to Roman Catholicism. If this were not so, he would not hesitate to unite with the faith he did consider best.

Protestants are able to be less intractable in regard to the religion of married partners and their children because (1) they do not regard marriage as a sacrament; (2) they interpret Christian marriage as involving more than the function of procreation; and (3) they are committed to the sacredness and dignity of the individual person.

Perhaps the different approach of Protestant and Roman Catholic clergy to these problems can be dramatized by setting the two in juxtaposition. An exchange of views between a Baptist pastor, Dr. Charles R. Bell, Jr., and a Jesuit priest, Father Warren C. Lilly, will be helpful. Dr. Bell had submitted certain proposals in regard to Protestant-Catholic marriage which impressed him as being fair and impartial—proposals which he believed might serve as a guide in mixed marriage situations. His proposals were three: (1) The wedding should always be held in the girl's church . . . neither party [should] have an unfair demand made upon him or her. . . . (2) The bride's pastor should officiate at the ceremony. . . . (3) Neither party should make a commitment of any kind, official or unofficial, other than the simple vow taken in that service."[1]

The reply by Father Lilly states the Roman Catholic objection to Dr. Bell's proposals and makes quite clear the difference in the Catholic view. Father Lilly writes:

If the marriage takes place before the Protestant minister, the Catholic is excommunicated. He is not married religiously or sacramentally. His family considers the marriage null and void. His church holds the contract invalid in the eyes of God. The Catholic himself is convinced of the nullity of his conjugal union. He has violated his conscience. He has repudiated his religion. He is desecrating his relations with the girl he has chosen as his wife. The more he respects her the more he is afflicted.[2]

What is in contrast here is not merely opposing ideas but two entirely different approaches to the problem. The Catholic view stands inflexibly on religious protocol. It says: "My church, right or wrong." The rights of an ecclesiastical organization must come ahead of all other considerations. The Protestant view leaves something to the individuals themselves. It refuses to confront them with inexorable "this or else" decrees but frankly respects their own capacity to work out their own problems, the religious problem included.

The Reformers

Neither of the great reformers, Martin Luther and John Calvin, regarded marriage as a sacrament. Protestants have generally agreed that it is not. That is, marriage is not one of those unique acts of worship in which the Holy Spirit is peculiarly operative. Marriage, in the view of the reformers, did not belong in the category with baptism and the Lord's Supper. Marriage was characteristic of societies other than Christian societies, hence could not be regarded as a Christian sacrament.

Roman Catholicism has a paradoxical teaching on this point. It holds that marriage is a sacrament, yet denies it to priests and nuns. Protestants hold that while marriage rites are not a Christian sacrament as such, the married state is willed and blessed by God. It is so desirable in his sight that all should be free to enter it, including clergymen.

Dr. Winfred E. Garrison has shown that in early Christian history the church regarded only baptism and the Lord's Supper as sacred rites conferring grace. Marriage was not included in the list of sacraments until the Middle Ages. "It was St. Bernard in the twelfth century who discovered that there ought to be exactly seven sacraments."[3] In keeping with their desire to return to original Christianity the reformers limited the sacraments to the two specifically enjoined by Christ himself.

In insisting that marriage was not a sacrament and that it had a civil significance apart from the church, the reformers did not intend to derogate its religious importance. Both Luther and Calvin taught that marriage was a divine ordinance, replete with spiritual benediction. The spirit of Luther's teaching is reflected in his reference to marriage as "a gift of God, the sweetest, the dearest, and the purest life above all celibacy and all singleness. . . ." *The Westminster Dictionary of Worship* (1645) insists that "although marriage be no sacrament nor peculiar to the Church of God but common to mankind and of public interest in every commonwealth, it is expected that marriage be solemnized by a lawful minister of the Word that he may counsel with the parties and pray for a blessing upon them."

Protestants have generally held that marriage is a natural contract as well as a spiritual one. For Christians, no less than for others, marriage should be under the jurisdiction of civil government. The Church of England holds that "marriage . . . both as a rite and as a state of life, is not something peculiarly Christian, but rather is an institution of the natural order which is taken into and sanctioned by the Christian Church." The state should not, of course, violate scriptural teaching in regard to marriage. Were it to do so, Christians should then oppose such a violation in conscience. They should oppose it just as they should oppose any act of the state which violated Christian conscience. They would have to say: "We must obey God rather than man." Yet this in no sense abrogates the state's proper jurisdiction over the marriage of citizens.

In Luther's time the Roman Church had not yet taken its inflexible position that every member in order to be validly married must be married before a priest. This development did not come until the Council of Trent (1545-63). Hence, Luther was not in disagreement with the teaching of the church at that time when he held that a couple could be validly married without a church ceremony at all. This remains the Protestant position today, though the Roman Catholic view now differs. Luther justified his view by arguing that marriage belonged to the realm of nature as well as of God. Pagans could be married as well as believers. Society had a concern of its own for all marriages, whether Christian or pagan.

The nice balance between the religious and the civil concerns in marriage is reflected in the Episcopal Address to the Methodist General Conference of 1960: "The church is, of course, not alone in her concern and responsibility for the home and family, but she has a particular ministry to perform because of her teaching concerning the sacred nature of marriage and the importance of the spiritual basis of home and family."

Spiritual Significance

The spiritual significance of marriage is emphasized in the stress which the *Methodist Discipline* places on proper preparation under the auspices of the church. Methodists are reminded that "marriage is an achievement. It doesn't just happen." There is a section on preparation for marriage which recommends "a regular course of instruction for youth on the Christian ideals of friendship, courtship, and marriage. . . ." Also recommended is adequate pastoral training for "premarital and postmarital counseling."

Protestants have consistently urged the desirability of

permanent marriage ties because this is both spiritually ennobling and socially desirable. No Protestant church takes the position that if one of its members is married by a clergyman of another denomination the marriage is invalid.

The entire Protestant emphasis on preparation for marriage and on premarital and postmarital counseling is designed to insure the permanence of the marriage tie. A Protestant pastor regards it as part of his responsibility to his parishioners to provide any assistance he can in preserving a marriage. He will not, however, insist that a divorce is evil under any and all conditions. There are occasions when divorce may actually be a lesser evil. There is no divine obligation to carry on a marriage which may entail large personality damage. This is especially true when there are children who may be adversely affected. A broken home always has unfortunate consequences for children, but an unbroken home, rife with dissension and bitterness, may be even worse. Protestants incline to make a judgment in light of the welfare of the family involved.

As to remarriage of divorced persons most Protestant churches exercise considerable caution. They do not, however, profess to enforce an absolute ban on such marriages. In 1956 the Protestant Episcopal Church took an action which in some respects "liberalized" its stand on remarriage of divorced persons. Previously the Episcopal Church had pursued a tight interpretation of Matthew 5:32: "Every one who divorces his wife, except on the ground of unchastity, makes her an adulteress; and whoever marries a divorced woman commits adultery (RSV)." This was interpreted to mean that the only divorced person who could be remarried in the church was the innocent party in a divorce that was granted on the ground of adultery.

The convention of the Protestant Episcopal Church in 1956 adopted a new rule. It provided for withdrawal of the church's recognition of a previous marriage in order to pave the way for remarriage of a divorced person in the church. This could only be done after a waiting period of at least a year and only on the basis of strictly limited circumstances. These circumstances were such as to render the previous marriage no true marriage and, therefore, not deserving of the church's blessing. One of the circumstances listed is this: "such defects of the personality as to make competent or free consent impossible." It is evident that this rule, like any other such rule, contains ambiguities. It could result in a wide variance of interpretation, depending on the predilections of the clergyman.

Protestant groups try to exercise caution and close surveillance in regard to divorced persons' seeking remarriage. They are primarily concerned with the question as to how well these persons are equipped for the marriage which they now propose to contract. Has their previous experience helped or hindered them in their quest of a successful marriage? The *Methodist Discipline* contains the following instruction to the clergy:

In view of the seriousness with which the Scriptures and the Church regard divorce, a minister may solemnize the marriage of a divorced person only when he has satisfied himself by careful counseling that: (a) the divorced person is sufficiently aware of the factors leading to the failure of the previous marriage, (b) the divorced person is sincerely preparing to make the proposed marriage truly Christian, and (c) sufficient time has elapsed for adequate preparation and counseling.

One of the greatest gains registered by Protestantism was its removal of the stigma attached to wedlock. During the period of Roman ascendency, the church had begun to teach that the state of virginity was morally superior to the married state. Indeed, the Roman Church still teaches that there are two acts which are religiously defiling to a priest. These are the shedding of blood and sexual intercourse. If either of these acts is performed by a priest, he must undergo a religious purification before he can give the sacrament again.

The Roman Church likewise holds that childbirth is defiling and requires the mother to undergo purification before she can receive the sacrament. Martin Luther was highly critical of this practice and did away with it. He taught that the sexual act in marriage was no more sinful than any other human act. No special onus was attached to it. The married state was, in fact, superior to virginity because it was more socially responsible. Luther declared that the church had no more right to forbid a man to marry than to forbid him to eat. To force a vow of chastity upon a person not equipped to receive it was simply to condemn that person to hell.

Luther's defense of married love is eloquent:

There are three kinds of love, false, natural, and married. False love is that which seeks its own, just as one loves gold, goods, honor, or women outside of matrimony contrary to God's command. Natural love is between father and children, brother and sister, et cetera. But above them all is married love, that is, a bride's love. It burns as fire, and seeks nothing more than the mate. It says, "I wish not yours, I wish neither gold nor silver, neither this nor that. I want only you. I want everything or nothing." All other loves seek something else than that which is love, but this love alone desires the beloved completely.[4]

Purpose of Marriage

While agreeing with the Roman Catholic position that procreation of children is a primary purpose of Christian marriage, Protestants have held that it has other purposes as well. Luther thought of marriage, for example, as a precaution against immorality as indicated in St. Paul's teaching that "it is better to marry than to burn" (1 Cor. 7:9). Luther pointed out that couples married without knowing whether they could have children or not and that it was perfectly proper for them to do so. Despite the absence of children, sex relations between husband and wife were a valid expression of their love and a protection against the evil of immorality.

Calvin saw in marriage the kind of companionship designed to bless and nurture man. The idea of companionship as equally significant with procreation led to an enhanced regard for the person in marriage. If companionship were of equal value with procreation, then the woman could hardly be regarded as a mere childbearing apparatus. Such a view would encourage her emergence as a person of value in her own right and as capable of a full share in the marriage partnership.

Calvin's teaching of companionship as a goal of Christian marriage has had a rich development in Protestant thought. The Federal (now National) Council of Churches in a statement issued by its Commission on Marriage and the Home, March, 1931, declared that relations between the marriage partners "have their source in the thought and purpose of God, first for the creation of human life, but also as a manifestation of divine concern for the happiness of those who have so wholly merged their lives." Here Christian concern in marriage goes far beyond any denominational concern. What is sought is not merely the procreation of persons who will be members of a church, but also the happiness and well-being of the partners themselves before God.

The inherent value of the married relationship for the two principals is reflected in Section V of the famous Lambeth Report (1958), which deals with "The Family in Contemporary Society." It asserts:

The Christian marriage relationship is a covenant, entered into with sacrifice in the joyful giving of each to the other; it is confirmed by the exchange of vows to which God's promised blessing is attached. . . . It is preserved by His (God's) forgiveness, it is enriched . . . by the Holy Spirit dwelling in the husband and wife as members of the Body of Christ, the Church.[5]

A statement by the General Assembly of the United Presbyterian Church, U.S.A. (May, 1959), goes even further in its recognition of the goal of companionship in Christian marriage. In this companionship the sexual tie plays a significant role.

In the wisdom of God Christian marriage is a relationship of love and fidelity which involves both companionship and parenthood, and . . . the sexual life within this relationship is given by God for the benefit of His children, and is neither an ethically neutral aspect of human existence, nor an evil which needs to be justified by something else, as, for an example, by the procreation of children.

This can hardly be called a movement "away from procreation" as the purpose of Christian marriage. It does, however, see a wider purpose, one which has regard for the persons of the partners and sees their relationship in terms of personal and mutual enrichment. The Lambeth Report holds that God's creative purpose is expressed as fully in the companionship of husband and wife as in procreation. The report identifies three primary aims that Christian marriage is to fulfil: procreation of children, fulfilment and completion of husband and wife, and the establishment of a stable environment for family life.

In Protestantism a great new dimension of meaning in the marriage tie is found in the concept of a spiritual enrichment and enhancement in human experience of the sex act. The act has meaning, not merely as procreation, which man shares with the animal, but also as love in all its ramifications. So Reinhold Niebuhr writes: "The prohibition of birth control assumes that the sexual function in human life must be limited to its function in nature, that of procreation. But it is the very character of human life that all animal functions are touched by freedom and released into more complex relationships."[6]

Respect for Personality

The pliability of Protestantism where mixed marriage is concerned, in contrast with the inflexibility of Roman Catholicism, is due, above all, to Protestant belief in the dignity and worth of the persons involved. Protestants regard persons before institutions. They would paraphrase Mark 2: 27: "Marriage is for persons, not persons for marriage." At no point does this difference show up more clearly than in attitudes toward child nurture. A prominent Protestant minister and an equally prominent Catholic priest recently engaged in a public controversy on this subject.

A correspondent of Norman Vincent Peale had written to inquire about how a Protestant should confront firm Catholic demands that all children born of the prospective union must be reared Catholic. Dr. Peale sought to cut the Gordian knot by submitting some practical and helpful proposals. He wrote: "I would maintain a scrupulously fair religious atmosphere in the home and, when the children are old enough, would let them decide their own religious faith for themselves. That is their right as sacred and sovereign personalities."[7]

Father Raymond J. Neufeld, who conducts a question-and-answer column for the Brooklyn *Tablet*, a Roman Catholic publication, had letters from his correspondents about Dr. Peale's answer. He commented:

He (the Protestant) will find that the Catholic Church asks another agreement of non-Catholics closely related to the first one, namely that they will do nothing to interfere with the practice of the Catholic party's faith. His Catholic wife will be obliged in conscience to have her children baptized as soon as possible in the one, true faith. If he refused to permit that Baptism, he is directly interfering with the practice of his wife's faith, he is depriving his children of their right to be baptized, and he might be responsible for a loss of faith in their entire lives.[8]

This is merely a reiteration of the Catholic thesis that the rights and the dogma of the Church as an institution must take precedence over any rights of the individuals involved.

Protestant concern is person-centered rather than institution-centered. Protestants would automatically place the children's welfare—physical, mental, moral, and spiritual—above any other consideration in the matter of their custody and upbringing. They would feel the same way in regard to subsequent custody arrangements as in regard to the prenuptial agreement. If a child were happy and well adjusted in his environment most Protestants would not think of disturbing him, even though he was being trained in a "wrong" religion. They would not permit a denominational

consideration to outweigh the sum total of factors constitut-
ing the child's welfare. To be specific, they would be un-
willing to remove a child whose natural parents were
Protestants from a Jewish couple with whom he was living
most happily.

If a child born of Protestant parents were to be brought
up in the Catholic faith, most Protestants would consider
this regrettable. But they would not consider it a matter
of such overriding concern as to warrant the dislocation and
disruption of the child in order to change it. They would
weigh the religious factor as a part of the total welfare of
the child. The child himself—all of him—would come first.

The Protestant clergyman interviewing a couple prior to
marriage will not attempt to dictate the terms. In case of a
difference in faith he will consider with them the problems
involved. He will not give them an ultimatum as to how
they must arrange their home religiously before he consents
to perform the ceremony. His refusal to dictate is prompted
not by any lack of conviction on his part but by respect
for the personalities involved. He does not refuse to
dictate because of any doubt in his own view as to what is
best, religiously, for the couple and their children. He refuses religious dictation on religious grounds. He refuses
to dictate because he believes that dictation in religion is
wrong. It would represent a desecrating intrusion upon
private judgment. Where matters as deeply personal as religious convictions are concerned one does not dictate.
Unless religion represents the free choice of persons it is
not religion. It simply cannot be coerced. Any religious
decision made under the duress of emotional and social
pressures will lack the approval of conscience and cannot
stand. The Protestant position, in extreme, can be stated
thus: Religiously speaking, the Protestant would rather leave

the individual "wrong" than coerce him into being "right."

The openness of the Protestant position is emphasized by Donald T. Erickson, a Baptist preacher, of Arlington, New Jersey, in a letter to the young people of his congregation:

Suppose you are deeply in love and already engaged to marry a Catholic. What then? Then you should insist on being married by a minister. Why? Because you do not have to sign away your children. We believe that parents should decide how their children are to be brought up. If you wish you can be married in a church. You will not be asked to sign any unfair agreement nor any agreement of any kind. And you may be buried together in any cemetery . . . without any question.

The Protestant minister will, as we have said, counsel with the couple about to be married on the whole question of proper Christian training for their children. It will be one of the major topics he will explore with them. But at no point will he demand of them specific commitments under threat of withdrawing from the service. Protestantism rests upon the voluntary principle of consent freely given.

The Protestant minister realistically recognizes that the attempt at clerical dictation fails more often than it succeeds. Roman Catholic authorities virtually acknowledge this when they admit that their church loses more children of mixed marriages than it holds. It is true that in the immediate context a clergyman may be able to manipulate the situation to the advantage of his church. By being articulately adamant and by throwing about his insistence an aura of finality and inevitability, he may be able to "win." But his triumph often proves to by a Pyrrhic one. In the long run the feeling of the home tends to recoil from his aggressiveness and to seek compensation in another direction.

The spirit of Protestantism at its best shines in these words of a Presbyterian parish minister, Dr. Richard H. Steiner:

A good Presbyterian is a Presbyterian because he believes that Presbyterianism represents more truthfully and accurately the mind and heart of Christ than does that sect known as the Disciples of Christ. Yet we are not so bigoted as to believe that the Disciples or the Unitarians or the Methodists or the Congregationalists are totally in error . . . ; and if a Unitarian young man falls in love with a Presbyterian young woman, Presbyterians do not insist that she be married in the Presbyterian church and that her children shall be taught Presbyterianism and be baptized by a Presbyterian minister.

Protestants bow to none in the urgency of their gospel and in the depth of their conviction. Yet for them freedom is a definitive value. With Protestants it is not the denomination that comes first; it is the person.

The Catholic
Antenuptial Agreement

4

The fundamental rule of the Roman Catholic Church governing the marriage of its members to Protestants is Canon Law 1012. It provides that for a Catholic no marriage ceremony can be valid except one performed by a Catholic priest. The other basic rule is Canon Law 1060, which forbids a Roman Catholic to marry a Protestant. When a Catholic desires to marry a Protestant, for what seem to be good reasons, the Church will grant a "dispensation" under which the priest can perform the rites. For a long time Catholic law provided that the unalterable requirement for such a dispensation was that the Protestant must convert to Roman Catholicism. But this was simply more than the traffic would bear. Hence, during the seventeenth century the Church began to grant dispensations without this requirement. In order to protect its interests, however, the Church then carefully specified additional requirements of the Protestant party. Every Roman Catholic diocese throughout the world has a written rule governing dispensations for marriage to a Protestant. This rule will have minor differences from diocese to diocese, but basically it is as follows:

Antenuptial Agreement

(To be signed by the non-Catholic party in a mixed marriage).

I, the undersigned, not a member of the Catholic Church, wishing to contract marriage with _____, a member of the Catholic Church, purpose to do so with the understanding that the marriage bond thus contracted is indissoluble except by death. I promise on my word and honor that I will not in any way hinder or obstruct the said _____ in the exercise of _____ religion and that all children of either sex born of our marriage shall be baptized and educated in the Catholic faith, and according to the teachings of the Catholic Church, even though said _____ should be taken away by death.

I further promise that I will marry _____ only according to the marriage rite of the Catholic Church; that I will not, either before or after the Catholic ceremony, present myself with _____ for marriage before a civil magistrate or minister of the gospel.

(Signature) _____

Signed in the presence of Rev. _____

Place _____ Date _____

Frequent Additions

There are a number of additions to the agreement which may be encountered in one diocese or another. One of the more popular additions requires the prospective Protestant spouse to take a six weeks' course in Roman Catholic doctrine, during which the priest attempts to convert him. Certain dioceses also add this rule: "In case of dispute (regarding custody of the children) I, furthermore, hereby fully agree that the custody of all the children shall be given to such guardians as to assure the faithful execution of this covenant and promise." Some dioceses in their statement of this provision actually stipulate that the bishop, as the representative of the Roman Catholic Church, be given "the right to enforce each and every promise herein contained in the event of the violation of the same by either party or both. . . ." This is a patent effort to give the Roman bishop dictatorial power over family arrangements and to enlist the power of civil authorities to make the agreement legally binding. Failing to secure enforcement of the antenuptial agreement, the bishop would theoretically have the power to step in and dissolve the marriage.

Another frequent addition to the agreement reads: "I will lead a married life in conformity with the teachings of the Catholic Church regarding birth control, realizing fully the attitude of the Catholic Church in this regard." Still further, the Roman Catholic party is often obligated to make a commitment to do all he or she can, prudently, for the conversion of the Protestant party.

Roman Catholic priests frequently lament the relative failure of their coercive tactics in mixed marriage, as we have seen in chapter one. Nevertheless, they frankly seek to use the emotional involvement of the Protestant as a means to bring about his conversion to Catholicism. The Jesuit, Father Daniel A. Lord, in his book *Questions I'm Asked About Marriage,* deals with the query of a girl who asks what he thinks of her prospects for marriage with a Protestant. "I am certain," she writes, "that after we are married I will be able to convert him." The priest answers:

If you are so certain that you can convert him, you will be wise to do so before you marry him. For then your marriage can be a Catholic marriage. . . . If you cannot convert him now, now that he is most in love with you and most eager to please you, what makes you think that you can convert him later? . . . Do your converting now.[1]

Failing to make a convert of the Protestant lover, the priests try to do the next best thing. They try to assure an airtight Catholic control of the marriage and the family. They strenuously seek to close every possible escape hatch. There is, nevertheless, always the dread possibility that one of the parties will change his mind or that, for some reason, the agreements, particularly concerning the children, will not be kept. If it can be shown that the Protestant party was "insincere" in making his commitment, or if he or she secretly exacted a contrary commitment from the Roman Catholic party, then the Roman Church can declare that the dispensation for the marriage was null and the marriage itself invalid.² This was so proclaimed by Pope Pius XI.

Protestant Reaction

The first point in the Roman Catholic agreement, the permanence of the marriage bond, is one in which Protestants would concur. Most Protestant services affirm the bond "until death us do part." The second, the promise not to obstruct the partner in his faith, is fair. What makes it a travesty is the counterpledge taken by the Catholic that he, or she, will do all in his power to convert the Protestant. Thus, the Protestant is inhibited in his expression of his faith while the Catholic is given the widest latitude. The third is the attempt by the Roman Church to monopolize for itself all the children. This attempt is the surest possible guarantee of dissension and strife in the marriage. The fourth is a final effort to eliminate any possibility of a Protestant clergyman's participating in the marriage service. The Roman Church contends that a Protestant ceremony would invalidate the Roman Catholic ceremony. It is determined to rule out any such solution.

It is hardly surprising that most Protestant churches have

reacted in vigorous hostility to the terms of this "agreement," which treats their faith and rites with contempt and seeks to eliminate them altogether from every mixed marriage. A few of their pronouncements, selected from many, are noted here. The Convention of the Protestant Episcopal Church resolved in 1949 that, "we assert that in no circumstances should a member of this church give any understanding, as a condition of marriage, that the children should be brought up in the practice of another communion." The Archbishop of York, the Most Reverend Cyril Forster Garbett, before his full synod, solemnly warned Anglicans against the Catholic antenuptial agreement. Said he:

I feel it necessary to warn Anglicans against signing this document, and to ask them to do their utmost to dissuade members of our Church from doing so. It means that Anglican fathers or mothers married to Roman Catholics are deprived of the right to influence the spiritual and religious upbringing of their children. It means disloyalty to the Church of their baptism and of their fathers. It is a humiliating condition. . . .[3]

The General Assembly of the Southern Presbyterian Church in 1959 sent to all its ministers a pastoral letter alerting them to the perils of Roman Catholic demands in mixed marriages. The letter declared:

Priding herself upon the rigid enforcement of her law, the Roman Catholic Church is relentless in this matter, with the result that there has been, and is, suffering and tragedy in many homes throughout our land. . . . We call upon our members to stand uncompromisingly in this matter, to resist resolutely this unfair demand, and refuse to make such a promise, especially in an hour when they are not truly free but are under the emotional compulsion of romantic love.

The Southern Baptist Convention endorsed a clear statement on the matter of Baptist-Catholic marriage in 1951. The messengers asserted that:

Our children should know the dangers of these promises so that they can take their stand as free, independent American citizens and refuse to make any promises that the Roman Catholic lover does not make. Marriage should not be a one-sided partnership where one gives up everything. It should be equal for both.

One of the strongest Protestant reactions to the Roman Catholic antenuptial agreement was registered by the congregation of Immanuel Lutheran Church of St. Charles, Missouri. It is in the form of a plan designed to reverse the situation of its members who have, prior to their marriage, unwittingly agreed to the Roman Catholic stipulations.' The plan, approved by a public resolution of this congregation, provides for the Protestant party to sign a second document in which he or she pledges not to carry out the terms of the contract imposed by the Roman Church.

There are seven "declarations" in which the penitent Protestant confesses his sin and shame at having signed such an agreement which is contrary to God's law and jeopardizes his own spiritual state. One of the declarations says plainly: "I declare that instead of keeping this promise (regarding the Catholic training of the children) I now break it and shall have my children baptized and reared in the Lutheran Church." The plan makes it clear that a member who refuses to sign such a declaration or fails to adhere to it is dropped from membership.

Concerning the Children

The principal indictment of the Roman Catholic agreement leveled by Protestant churches relates to its demands concerning the religious training of the children. The right of the children to self-determination in the matter of religion is a right precious to Protestants. The Catholic agreement is seen by Protestants as an effort to freeze the religious loyalties of children via a contract drawn and signed before they are ever conceived. It is an effort to set these loyalties irrevocably to the religion of one of the parents and to the exclusion of the other.

For a long time Christians have condemned the evils of child marriage as practiced in certain non-Christian lands. This is the arrangement by which children little more than infants are betrothed by the action of adults. When they have attained sufficient age they are brought together and the marriage is consummated without their ever having an opportunity to discover whether they like each other or not. Such arrangements have been widely condemned as a violation of human rights and an affront to the dignity and sacredness of the individuals involved.

It appears to many Protestants that the stipulations concerning children demanded by Roman Catholic priests offer a close analogy to the practice of child marriage. For here it is proposed to sign away not the mere right to a choice of a marriage partner but the choice of religious faith itself. The practitioners of child marriage do not proceed with their arrangements until after the child is born. But in the Roman Catholic agreement the individual's sacred right, under God, to choose his faith is taken from him before he even comes into the world. Granted that such a program fails more often than it succeeds, it does succeed in many instances. There is one question which lies at the heart of the Protestant protest: Is this a moral program? Do persons—any persons, even parents—have a right to do this to unborn children? Protestants, with their unfaltering emphasis upon the individual and the significance of his moral choice, would answer no.

There is a further indictment of the Catholic antenuptial agreement. This is made often enough by Protestants, but it can also be shared by the Orthodox Church, Jews, and members of all other faiths. It declares that the agreement is out of place in a free, democratic society. It is of supreme importance that the Roman Catholic hierarchy be made to feel the weight and cogency of this contention.

The argument is advanced by the Roman Catholic hierarchy, and even supported in some Protestant circles, that this church has the right to make any rules it wants to in regard to the marriage of its own members. The Protestant contemplating marriage with a Roman Catholic does not *have* to sign the contract if he does not want to. Therefore, his freedom cannot be jeopardized. This defense of the Catholic position does not quite cover the ground. In the first place, let it be made clear that a church is *not* altogether free to make rules, even for its own members, in regard to marriage. This is not because the state is superior to the church; it is because the state must fulfil its role as conserver of the general health and well-being of the people and also as "arbiter among the sects."

A century ago Mormons in the West had a denominational rule which permitted polygamy and they practiced this form of marriage widely. It was argued with considerable eloquence that the Mormons were a peaceable, thrifty people and that under the terms of religious liberty they should be free to make their own marriage rules. This logic was rejected by the United States Supreme Court in

Reynolds vs. *United States*[5] and *Davis* vs. *Besson.*[6] It abrogated this particular marriage rule of a religious denomination and in so doing declared:

Marriage, while from its very nature a sacred obligation, is, nevertheless, in most civilized nations, a civil contract, and usually regulated by law. Upon it society may be said to be built, and out of its fruits spring social relations and social obligations and duties, with which government is necessarily required to deal.

It seems evident that the marriage rules of any church must not fail to take into account the nature of the society in which that church exists. After all, marriage is necessarily social as well as religious in its nature. It is socially disruptive for one religious group to make marriage rules which are unfair and oppressive to members of other groups. Common sense adjustment of its denominational rules in the light of social necessity is a part of the price a church pays for its existence in a pluralistic society.

In a free, democratic society rules of the state in regard to marriage, or in regard to anything else, are not arbitrary decrees of a dictator but represent the will of the people. In no area, including that of marriage, can the rights of all the people suffer curtailment by a discriminatory marriage plan imported to this country from nations where canon laws have governed such matters. The indispensable condition of peace among the churches and in society generally is that there be reciprocity among religious groups in regard to marriage. That is, the marriage ceremony of each must be regarded by the others as binding even upon its own members. To persist in a denominational derogation of the marriage services of other churches is to derogate marriage itself and to undermine the foundations of society.

It is all very well to insist that "divine law" cannot yield to social convenience on a matter of conviction. But a particular rendering of "divine law" which works hardship on persons of many faiths cannot be accorded uncritical acceptance by an entire society. There are different interpretations of "divine law" by other groups within that society. One of these groups, however resolute and powerful, cannot be permitted to impose its will upon all. The Federal Council of Churches as early as 1932 made the clearest possible pronouncement on this subject:

No religious body which confesses itself Christian can tolerate the imposition upon one of its own members of the requirements of another religious body by which the religious scruples of the member are aroused, or action repugnant to reason and conscience is forced upon him by an authority which he does not acknowledge. . . . If either enters upon the union as a propagandist, determined through the intimacies of marriage to subvert the religious faith of the other, disaster is imminent.[7]

What the Council was saying was not only that such coercive tactics are religiously outrageous but also that they are socially disruptive. The democratic society which prevails in the United States has rejected the Roman Catholic rules on mixed marriage by refusing to make them legally binding on citizens. But more than this tacit rejection is needed. The moral climate of public opinion should be directed against this unjust and un-American instrument of clerical power. All Protestant groups must continue to register their rejection of it in the strongest possible terms and to encourage their members to implement this rejection by all available means.

Time for a Change

One of the most encouraging aspects of the struggle for inter-creedal justice in marriage procedures is the attitude of Catholic laymen. As we have already seen, there are as many Protestant-Catholic marriages performed outside the Roman Church as in it. This means that half the Catholics involved in these marriages are either in revolt against the priest's stipulations or indifferent to them. Widespread disregard of this impossible code for mixed marriages would be a long step toward its abandonment.

Certainly every Protestant who is a prospect for a mixed marriage should insist, in good humor but with firmness, on the observance of fair play in the marriage arrangements. For example, if he, or she, is to take a course in Roman Catholic doctrine, then it would be only fair for the Catholic to make some study of the particular Protestant faith involved. While the priest might forbid such a turnabout, it is basic to fair play and should be insisted upon.

If the priest seems inclined to dictate and prescribe for the couple, he should be advised that this is unwelcome. He should be freely admitted to the discussions in his proper role of adviser and instructor. But he is not a dictator and any attempt on his part to become one should be firmly rejected. Decisions in regard to the marriage should be made by the couple and by them alone. But they should be decisions made in the full light of freedom and information.

Protestants, and Catholics as well, are sometimes inclined to view Roman Catholic practice as an immutable law, like that of the Medes and Persians, which is incapable of change. Priests are fond of fostering this belief. Other churches can and do change their rules and procedures, but the Roman Church never changes. This is a false impression.

The Roman Church has changed its marriage rules any number of times in the past and is quite capable of changing them again. For example, this church insisted for centuries that Protestant ministers had no right to marry anybody, that this was a privilege solely reserved to Roman Catholic priests. What broke this rule down and changed it was the vast ignoring of it in practice. When whole nations became populated with "illegitimate" persons and the number of nonpriest marriages topped the priestly ones, then the Roman Church decided that baptized Protestants could marry validly before their ministers.[8] Theoretically, the pope could at any time resume full control of all marriages and decree that to be valid they must be performed by priests of his own church. This is unlikely, however, in view of the prevailing climate of public opinion.

A corresponding change must be brought about in the same way in regard to the Roman Catholic antenuptial agreement. The massive resistance program already under way should be consciously strengthened and buttressed at every possible point. The chances are that if the disregard of the priests' demands, already widespread, could be augmented to any substantial degree, another reappraisal of Roman Catholic law would become necessary.

A change in Roman Catholic procedures is imperative if Catholics and Protestants are to exist peaceably in this democratic society. Reinhold Niebuhr has discussed the nature of the democratic toleration which is necessary among us: "Some of the greatest perils to democracy arise from the fanaticism of moral idealists who are not conscious of the corruption of self-interest in their professed ideals. Democracy therefore requires something more than a religious devotion to moral ideals. It requires religious humility."[9]

The Roman Catholic antenuptial contract is a convincing example of the kind of behavior which may represent a commendable cultist zeal but which in a pluralistic society is simply untenable. After all, the Roman Catholic people are a part, and an important part, of our democratic society. They cannot live in an isolated enclave. Since they are, like Protestants, a constituent element of the American community, interfaith marriages are inevitable. The current terms which the hierarchy sets for such unions are impossible terms. They must be reappraised in the light of our common mandate to live together in peace.

Birth Control

5

The Roman Catholic ban on birth control for its own members, and even for the members of other churches when it can achieve it, constitutes a major impediment to a successful Protestant-Catholic marriage. The ban dates from two papal decrees, March 21, 1851 and April 10, 1853.

The irrevocable decision which doomed the Roman Church to at least a century of opposition to birth control was, however, taken by Pius XI in 1930. His denunciation as set forth in the *Encyclical on Christian Marriage* contains the following language:

In order that she may preserve the chastity of the nuptial union from being defiled by this foul strain, the Church raises her voice in token of her divine ambassadorship and through Our mouth proclaims anew: any use whatsoever of matrimony exercised in such a way that the act is deliberately frustrated in its natural power to generate life is an offense against the law of God and of nature, and those who indulge in such are branded with the guilt of a grave sin.[1]

There is reported to have been serious opposition within the ranks of the clergy, particularly among the French, to any such dogmatic pronouncement of the Roman Church.

The Pope went through with it, nevertheless, and put his church in such an insupportable position that some of its wiser leaders have been searching feverishly ever since for a graceful way out.

Lest there be any doubt as to the application of this principle to American Catholics, the bishops of the United States hierarchy issued in November, 1959, a statement reiterating their church's traditional stand and specifically denouncing the Protestant theology "which envisages artificial birth prevention within the married state as the 'will of God.'" They even went so far as to forbid their members to support any government-sponsored program of birth control, whether domestic or foreign. They said: "(United States Catholics) will not support any public assistance, either at home or abroad, to promote artificial birth prevention . . . whether through direct aid or by means of international organizations."² The ban was based on the contention that birth control constitutes a violation of the "natural law" and defeats procreation which God has willed to be the purpose of marriage. Those who made use of birth control were declared by the Pope to be guilty of "grave sin," thus requiring confession and penance.

The strict prohibition of birth control with its disastrous consequences for happiness in marriage and for a world about to blow up with its birth explosion, is rooted in an incomplete theology of marriage. If procreation of children is the sole purpose of the sexual act, it follows that any program which derails the act from this particular accomplishment is sinful. With the possible exception of the so-called "rhythm method" of birth control, the only alternative the Roman Catholic Church can offer to the "fertility cult" of marriage is continence. Bishop G. Bromley Oxnam once computed that given a woman's childbearing years as twenty-five, and the normal family as three to six children, this would be tantamount to recommending continence for about twenty of the twenty-five years.[3]

Possibly in deference to Protestants, Pius XI sought scriptural justification for the rule against contraceptives in an obscure Old Testament story (Gen. 38:9-10), which really has nothing to do with the matter.[4] It is a story about Onan whose brother had died and left a widow. According to the Hebrew law, the surviving brother was then required to cohabit with the widow in order to preserve the name and lineage of his brother and also certain property rights. Onan selfishly objected to the performance of his traditional duty. He began but did not complete the sexual act with the widow. Thereupon, he was punished with death. It is quite clear that the ancient story is not concerned with birth control at all. It is concerned with the importance of preserving unbroken the line of family succession. Since Onan's brother had died without issue, Onan's obligation to the widow and to the family lineage was clear. He was punished with death, not because he practiced birth control, but because he failed to meet his responsibility to his brother and the clan. That this story, rooted in ancient Hebrew culture, could become justification for a perpetual ban on contraception strains both credulity and imagination.

Obsession with procreation as the sole object of both marriage and sex relations has led the Roman Catholic Church into its impossible position on birth control. In the face of the population explosion, this position demands resolute refusal to face what may be the gravest single marital problem. Protestants have been able to avoid this pitfall by virtue of a wider concept of marriage. They have regarded marriage as being not only for procreation but also for the well-being of the partners themselves.

Perils of Infallibility

The ineffectual stand of the Roman Catholic Church in regard to birth control is a convincing demonstration of the perils of "infallibility" in moral matters. When a person makes a mistake he can correct it and go on. When a government makes a mistake it can reverse its policy. But when an "infallible" church makes a mistake, what can it do? It is stuck with the mistake. It must change, yet it cannot change. Originally, many Protestant churches took the same position on birth control as the Roman Catholic Church. But not professing to carry the burden of "infallibility" they were able to reverse themselves and take a position in line with the facts and the needs of the present day.

In the fall of 1959 the Columbia Broadcasting System presented over a nation-wide hookup a telecast dealing with the worldwide population explosion and the need for birth control. Dr. Theodore M. Hesburgh, president of the University of Notre Dame, defended the Roman Catholic ban on birth control in the face of the appalling worldwide demonstration of its need. With considerable eloquence, Dr. Hesburgh contrasted the position of the Roman Church with that of the Church of England. He quoted the original pronouncements of the Church of England against birth control; next he quoted recent pronouncements of the same church which favored it. Then he triumphantly cited the position of the Roman Catholic Church which had maintained the same position without change. Quite without realizing it, Father Hesburgh had leveled a terrific indictment against his own church. None could have indicated more eloquently than he that the dangerous weakness of the Roman Catholic Church is precisely this inability to change its position when a new day and new conditions make it imperative to do so. This is particularly true when it takes a position on a matter of medical science and vast sociological concern.

The Roman Catholic Church is almost desperately endeavoring to retreat from its untenable stand on birth control by singling out for its approval one particular method called the "rhythm method." The rhythm method differs from some other methods in that it relies not upon contraception but upon timing intercourse to so-called "safe periods" when conception cannot take place. The principal difference between the "rhythm method" and standard, medically approved procedures is that rhythm is notoriously unreliable. The trouble with it is that very few women have the complete regularity of menstrual periods which is an indispensable requirement for success. Dr. Alan F. Guttmacher, nationally known obstetrician and authority on birth control, commenting on the difference in effectiveness of the two methods, has said:

The best evidence we have is that the failure rate among couples who practice rhythm is *two to three times higher than among those who use medical methods of contraception.* Pope Pius XII himself conceded this when he expressed hope that "science will succeed in providing this licit method with a sufficiently secure basis."[5]

We have often heard marriage partners complain bitterly about the failure of the Catholic-approved method. Never have we heard it endorsed as reliable. Many have found it a way to prompt pregnancy. The Roman Catholic hierarchy has singled out this unfortunate method of birth control for its approval because it employs no device and, therefore, offers a technical argument that it is "natural" rather than "artificial." Thus, Catholic dogma is not violated.

But to the intelligent judgment of millions there is no moral superiority of one birth control method over another. The point is to find a reliable method and to use it judiciously—not to prevent births but to space them intelligently.

High hopes were entertained when the contraceptive pill called Envoid was recently perfected and placed on the market. At least, it was felt, a safe method of birth control had been developed which would meet with Roman Catholic approval. No contraceptive device was involved in the method—nothing but the pill. While certain Roman Catholic laymen spoke approvingly of the pill, it has now, unfortunately, been denounced by the Church. *The Catholic Marriage Manual,* for example, bearing the imprimatur of Cardinal Spellman and used as a standard item in preparation for thousands of Roman Catholic marriages, contains the following: " 'Birth control' is a misnomer . . . where the so-called 'birth control pills' are used. Taken by mouth, their purpose is the prevention of ovulation and thus of conception. Such pills are artificial means of preventing births and, as such, are immoral."[6]

A tragic aspect of the Roman Catholic rule, barring sound birth control procedures, is that it was made and enforced by bachelors. It seems almost fantastic that the law denying such procedures to millions of American women was promulgated by a celibate priest living in Rome. The Church thus attempts to thrust Catholic laymen into the extremely unfortunate position of having to obey the priests' dictation in this matter, or being dropped from good standing. For Roman Catholic women who believe themselves bound by such directives we can have appropriate pity. But for Protestant women whom that Church attempts to bring under the rule via mixed marriage, a stronger emotion is needed. Protestant women will do well to firmly reject this obscurant marriage rule and to be guided by the wisdom of their own church.

The Protestant Partner

The Roman Catholic prohibition of birth control by "artificial" means is imposed upon the Protestant partner in a mixed marriage. It may be done by means of a direct commitment demanded by the priest as a condition of his performing the marriage ceremony. The standard practice, however, is to impose it on the Protestant by way of the Catholic partner. This is done in the confessional. He or she may be asked point-blank by the confessor whether contraception is being used. If he, or she, acknowledges such use, then this constitutes a state of mortal sin and the guilty party must be absolved by repenting and performing a suitable penance. Repentance must, of course, include desisting from the "sin" of using contraceptives. Thus, if the Catholic partner simply confesses this "sin" on each occasion and gets absolution, this practice will be ruled out on the ground that his confession is not sincere. If, on the other hand, he reasons that it is his own business and says nothing to the priest, then, since he concealed his "sin," his confession is held to be invalid. If he takes communion under these circumstances he is supposedly in a state of "mortal sin."

The Roman Catholic rule on birth control imposes a severe strain on the marriage relationship, particularly in a Protestant-Catholic marriage. If we ignore the rhythm method—and probably it ought to be ignored—the couple is confronted with the dilemma of a long period of abstinence or a "baby-a-year" program. The intolerable frustration makes the former psychologically impossible; the crush-

ing weight of responsibility for the care and education of un-
limited children makes the latter impossible. If the Roman
Catholic insists on planning his family intelligently, scien-
tifically spacing and limiting his children to the three or
four he can properly train and educate, he is likely to suffer
harassment from his church. How much will depend on the
attitude of the particular confessor, we do not know. But
the fact is that the confessor has been trained to be inexorable on this matter.

Protestant and Catholic Views Opposed

Protestant churches and the Roman Catholic Church are
almost diametrically opposed on issues concerning the
spacing of children through birth control. Most of the
Protestant groups strongly endorse and support what the
Roman Catholic Church flatly forbids. The National Presbyterian Church, Washington, D.C., in the case of every
marriage performed by one of its ministers, has a congregational rule, endorsed by its session, which requires complete
counseling on the proper spacing and limitation of children,
including methods of birth control. The premarital counseling of the Catholic priest would be directly opposed since
the priest would warn against the very procedures the
Presbyterian minister would recommend.

Richard M. Fagley, executive secretary of the Commission of the Churches on International Affairs, established
by the World Council of Churches and the International
Missionary Council, has provided an excellent summary of
the stand taken by most of the major Protestant bodies
concerning family planning and birth control.[7] The
Augustana Evangelical Lutheran Church in 1954 stressed
proper spacing of children and the right of the child to love,
nurture, and care. The resolution declared:

So long as it causes no harm to those involved, either immediately or over an extended period, none of the methods for controlling the number and spacing of births of children has any special moral merit or demerit. It is the spirit in which the means is used, whether it is "natural" or "artificial," which defines its "rightness" or "wrongness." "Whatsoever ye do, do all to the glory of God" (1 Cor. 10:31) is a principle pertinent to the use of the God-given reproductive power.

The Evangelical and Reformed General Synod of 1947, out of a concern to strengthen family life, endorsed the principle of wise family planning through appropriate medical aid. The *Discipline of the Methodist Church*, 1956, asserts that "we believe that planned parenthood, practiced in Christian conscience, may fulfil rather than violate the will of God." The Anglican Church has done important work in recovering an understanding of God's creative purpose in the relationship of husband and wife, a purpose in juxtaposition with the procreation of children but distinct from it. In connection with this view, the Anglican Church has approved judicious and responsible use of contraception by its members. The Lambeth Report contains a statement which offers valuable insight into the Christian implications of birth control:

A knowledge of the relation of sexual love to the procreative process gives to a couple the power, and therefore the responsibility, to lift the begetting of children out of the realm of biological accident of "fate" into the realm of personal decision—which is also the realm of grace, where man is free to wait upon God and consciously to respond to His will. Carried further, it enables husband and wife to decide, within the providence of God, whether any one act of intercourse shall be for the enrichment of expression of their personal relationship only, or for the begetting of children also.

The United Presbyterian Church in a statement approved by its General Assembly in 1959, resolved that "the proper use of medically approved contraceptives may contribute to the spiritual, emotional, and economic welfare of the family." The United Lutheran Church in 1956 lent official approval to a statement which said: "Irresponsible conception of children up to the limit of biological capacity and selfish limitation of children are equally detrimental. Choice as to means of contraceptive control should be made upon professional medical advice."

The most definitive Protestant pronouncement on birth control since Lambeth was that of the National Council of Churches issued February 23, 1961. Its key sentence reads: "Most of the Protestant churches . . . believe that couples are free to use the gifts of science for conscientious family limitation provided the means are mutually acceptable, non-injurious to health, and appropriate to the degree of effectiveness required in the specific situation."[8]

The Roman Catholic distinction between so-called "artificial" and "natural" methods of birth control is considered and rejected by Protestant authorities. Lambeth declared that "there seems to be no more distinction between the means now known and practiced, by the use whether of estimated period of infertility, or of artificial barriers to the meeting of sperm and ovum—or, indeed, of drugs which would, if made effective and safe, inhibit or control ovulation in a capable way."

Outstanding Protestant theologians of the twentieth century, Karl Barth and Reinhold Niebuhr, have flatly rejected the Roman Catholic position on birth control. Barth, in particular, has no patience with the elaborately drawn distinctions between different methods. All known methods have disadvantages, he thinks. Some have more disadvantages than others, but he finds that all are *morally* on the same basis. Husband and wife should assess their problem and make their own decision as to method without outside pressure.

The fallacy in the Roman Catholic argument for a "moral distinction" between birth control methods is succinctly disposed of by Dr. Otto A. Piper. He writes:

The moral question is not whether a Christian has a right to use contraceptives but rather whether he is allowed to interfere at all with the process of fertilization in the act of sexual intercourse. It should be obvious that the ethical issue is not dependent on the means used for that end. For whether conception is prevented by the use of contraceptives, or by the interruption of the sexual act, or by limiting intercourse to safe days, there is an evident action of the will whose purpose is to prevent conception.[9]

Protestant-Catholic differences on birth control have come to a head in Connecticut. This state has a law which forbids dissemination of information on birth control under any circumstances. The law applies to everyone, including physicians and ministers. While not generally enforced, it is kept on the books by the political action of the Catholic bishops who have on many occasions prevented its repeal. Seven lawsuits were filed in Connecticut to challenge the constitutionality of this law. One of the more interesting suits was filed by three clergymen, Dr. George Teague, a Methodist; Dr. C. Lawson Willard, an Episcopalian; and Dr. Luther Livingston, a Lutheran. They contended that they were "bound by the teachings of the church and their own religious beliefs to counsel married parishioners on the use of contraceptive devices and to give such advice in premarital counseling." This meant, they said, that the

Connecticut law deprived them of their religious liberty as guaranteed under the First and Fourteenth Amendments.

Since Connecticut and Massachusetts are the only two states which have such specific interference with family and religious liberty in their laws, the test in Connecticut was watched with interest. One of the cases finally reached the United States Supreme Court in 1961. The suit was one brought by Dr. C. Lee Buxton, the noted gynecologist of Yale, and two women identified merely as Mrs. Poe and Mrs. Doe. Mrs. Poe had had three consecutive pregnancies terminating in the birth of abnormal children who died. Mrs. Doe in her last pregnancy remained unconscious for two weeks. Physicians agreed that another such experience would kill her. The plaintiffs asked a declaratory judgment outlawing the Connecticut law which brands them as criminals for giving and receiving contraceptive information in these circumstances.

The Supreme Court in a shaky five to four decision refused to upset the Connecticut law. The nature of the decision seems to indicate, however, that the law is doomed. The court refused to meet the issue head on because the Connecticut law was not actually being enforced. It was, in fact, being quite openly violated throughout the state. The court pointed out that no one had been jailed or fined for violation of this law and that, therefore, the case was unrealistic. The court, in effect, invited a new suit with a less abstract fact situation. A birth control clinic has now begun to operate openly in the state in the hope that officials will make arrests. If they do so, it seems a virtual certainty that the case will go to the Supreme Court with a rather clearly indicated outcome.[10]

The National Council of Churches has spoken out unequivocally against antibirth control laws like those of

Connecticut and Massachusetts: "For most couples family planning requires access to appropriate medical information and counsel. Legal prohibitions against impartation of such information and counsel violate the civil and religious liberties of all citizens including Protestants."

Signs of Hope

The position which the Roman Catholic Church has assumed on birth control appears to be hopelessly intransigent. Yet the situation is not nearly so dark as it might appear. What is patently taking place in this church is a "human adjustment" to the clerics' impossible demands. Surveys taken among Roman Catholic laymen consistently indicate that they are, in considerable numbers, refusing to obey their church in this matter. Msgr. Irving A. DeBlanc, director of the National Catholic Family Life Bureau, reported to his organization's convention in June, 1960, that a number of recent studies showed that Roman Catholic married couples use contraceptive birth control "in about the same measure" as Protestant and Jewish couples.[11] This situation Msgr. DeBlanc described as "alarming, arresting, and provocative." The studies indicate, he reported, that many Catholics "follow the influence of their neighbors and do not take their cues for behavior from a divinely inspired Church."

The direction that Protestant-Catholic action should take in regard to the priests' ban on birth control is evident from Msgr. DeBlanc's analysis. Instead of supine acceptance of an absurd and impossible rule, there should be forthright rejection of it by all concerned. There is one form of opposition which outmoded rules of the Roman Catholic Church have never been able to stand against. This is massive resistance. Deprived of the powers of police coercion, the hierarchy can rely only on moral suasion. When this is firmly rejected by considerable numbers of its people, including those involved in mixed marriages, the rule will simply have to give way.

There are other features of Roman Catholic marriage regulations which can create serious trouble in a Protestant-Catholic marriage. One which must be mentioned is a feature of the Catholic medical code which absolutely forbids therapeutic abortion, performed in unusual circumstances when necessary to save the life of a mother.[12] Very rarely a situation will present itself in which it becomes evident that both the mother and the unborn child cannot survive. Yet occasionally this very predicament does come about. When it occurs the Roman Catholic directive to physicians and to Catholic hospitals where their medical code must be enforced is very clear: "Direct abortion is never permitted, even when the ultimate purpose is to save the life of the mother." Conservative estimates place the number of American mothers who die unnecessarily each year because of this rule at one thousand to two thousand. This is admittedly a small number, but when it happens once it is too much.

The moral choice between the life of the mother and the life of the child, when it must be made in just these terms, is exceedingly difficult. One Catholic authority, Donald T. Mather, avoids the dilemma by denying that it ever exists.[13] Yet the predisposition must certainly be in favor of the mother. She is a mature person who has already formed a considerable number of significant social relationships that would be disrupted by her death. Particularly is this true when she has other children who would be bereft of her care. Here she stands in contrast with the child who has formed no relationships as yet and has not even been born.

An obvious form of action against this rule suggests itself. If the woman is being attended in her pregnancy by a Roman Catholic physician, his attitude on this particular rule of his church should be learned. Also, if the mother plans to go to a Catholic hospital, inquiry should be made to see whether the dangerous denominational rule in question must be obeyed. The fact is that every Roman Catholic hospital is declared to be bound by the official Catholic rules of medical practice, the ban on all therapeutic abortion included. If the hospital in question is an exception, this should be clearly noted. If the assurance is not forthcoming the mother should be taken to another hospital, even at considerable sacrifice. Here, as in connection with other Roman Catholic rules that are unreasonable and disruptive, forthright resistance by both Protestant and Catholic partners is indicated. In any event, the choice of obstetrician and hospital should be left to the wife.

Living with It

6

"We can work out the religious differences because we're in love." Famous last words! The answer might well be: "That's the reason you can't work it out." Love may obscure the problems of a Protestant-Catholic marriage for the time being, but it can never solve them. Love is a paradox. It entices young persons into a marriage beset with complex problems. Then it renders the solution of these problems difficult, if not impossible. Love is the sweet ensnarer and the drugged potion.

A well-nigh irresistible emotional surge impels two young persons to merge their lives in matrimony. Yet the emotional urge is the very factor which blunts reason and judgment when they are most needed. No relationship on earth demands a more serious and cautious appraisal than marriage. But persons in love are usually incapable of thinking objectively about it. During courtship the emotional factor may be decisive and engulfing, obliterating all other considerations. After a few years of marriage, love, in seemingly perverse reversal, commences to accentuate what it had hitherto obscured. Particularly is this true in problems relating to religious differences.

Religion has deep emotional roots; so also has love. Two flammable elements with the potential of an explosion when combined! For it is the nature of love that each, loving the other, wants the other to be like him or her. This is true of husband and wife; it is true of parent and child. During the courtship all this may be obscured; or if not obscured, then failed to be seen in anything like a proper perspective. It is almost as certain as Boyle's law that ten years of married life will bring to focus every problem which existed potentially at the time the vows were said. This may be too bad but it is also too true.

What really lies at the heart of the problem is a fundamental spiritual difference—two sharply divergent ways of thinking and acting. Perhaps one of the finest descriptions of this difference comes from a young Catholic husband who was doing some soul-searching as a result of his mixed marriage:

There is such a thing as the Catholic mind and there is a very definite Protestant mind, and the twain, I fear, shall never meet. In the Catholic mind there is an authoritarian attitude in religious questions. . . . In the Protestant, there is an individualistic attitude. . . . These attitudes color a person's way of looking at the most commonplace objects. The two minds can respect each other and they can try to understand, but they have very little success.

The Religious Problem

For the Roman Catholic partner, as for the Protestant, a mixed marriage carries a heavy religious entailment. This is especially true of the Catholic who has defied the rulers of his church and has been married by a Protestant minister. Here the entailment may be so great as to strain the marriage tie beyond the breaking point. In cases where a Catholic has been married by a Protestant minister and the children of the union are being reared in the Protestant faith, the entire weight of Catholic teaching and practice will be thrown against such arrangements and, if the arrangements persist, against the marriage itself.

If the Catholic has any contact with his church at all, no occasion will be lost to remind him that the marriage he has "attempted" is not a valid marriage in the eyes of his church, that he must be regarded as "living in sin," and that his children are in dubious state. Unless the person is unusually tough-minded and resilient, this weight of ecclesiastical opinion is bound to affect him in time. The case of the parochial school product is especially difficult, for these very ideas have been carefully instilled in his mind during his most impressionable years. If he begins to inquire around in his "sinful" situation to see what he can do toward getting his marriage "blessed," he may be told as one such inquirer was: "That expression *to get their marriage blessed* is a mistake and a misnomer . . . . It should never be used. In the first place, the couple who have gone to the justice of the peace or a minister are not yet married. There is no marriage to be blessed."[1]

The kind of pressure which the Roman Catholic hierarchy is capable of exerting against a member who has violated its marriage rules is indeed formidable. A Catholic family and Catholic friends often serve the hierarchy's ends by exerting their own pressures against the couple.

Being deeply in love with wife or husband, the Catholic for a considerable time may be able to resist this attritive pull on his marriage. But the Church never tires. She keeps the pressure on, well knowing that in the long run the odds are in her favor. In an astonishing number of cases she is able to bring the recalcitrant to heel.

Peter, a Roman Catholic, had been happily married to

Susan, a Protestant, for fourteen years. There had been a Protestant ceremony and three children born of the union had been reared Protestant. The man was deeply in love with his wife and devoted to his children. Yet the combined pressures of his church and his family proved more than he could take. A highly intelligent man, he had initially rejected the thought that he was "living in sin" as absurd and even amusing. Yet, under constant goading from various quarters, the matter did begin to prey upon his mind. Finally, Peter was broken down. He began pleading with his wife to be remarried by a priest and make the concessions in regard to the Catholic training of the children. This she refused to do, pointing out how completely disruptive it would now be for the children. Failing to move her, Peter eventually separated and persuaded Susan to get a divorce. Then he married again, with the full blessing of his church, and is now engaged in the process of begetting and rearing a Catholic family.

The Catholic Conscience

The Protestant simply has no counterpart to this kind of pressure in the whole range of his religious experience. In this realm he stands alone with his conscience before God. Now to be sure this can be an awful mastery in itself. There are times when conscience speaks so imperatively that the one to whom it speaks can only obey, even though the cost be great. Recall Martin Luther at Worms: "Here I stand. I can do no other. God help me. Amen!" When the voice of conscience speaks loud and clear within, its command is apt to be stronger than that of any external authority. When, then, these two authorities clash, as they have been known to do in a Protestant-Catholic marriage, the marriage itself may be shaken.

The voice of authority with which the Roman Catholic hierarchy speaks to its members is not to be confused with the "voice of conscience," as Protestants understand it. The voice which commands the Catholic layman is the voice of an apparatus. It claims, to be sure, to be God's only constituted apparatus and to speak with divine authority. The Protestant does not share this view. To him the Catholic priests appear as dictators demanding obedience to their rules under the gravest threats. To the Protestant these rules are not interior imperatives of the spirit. They are external coercion. The enforcement of these rules in marriage is not "deep calling to deep"; it is priestly class exerting its rule upon its subjects.

The external nature of a Catholic conscience is well illustrated by the reply of a priest to a question on this subject. The questioner wanted to know what a Roman Catholic would do in case of a conflict between the dictates of his own conscience and the dictates of his church. Father John V. Sheridan promptly replied:

There is no conflict between the dictates of a Catholic's conscience and those of his church for the simple reason that the dictates of his conscience will always follow and reflect those of his church. . . . Catholic Church members' consciences are actually formed by the decrees of the Church.[2]

A Roman Catholic magazine prints a letter purportedly found in the drawer of a lapsed Catholic after her death of cancer. The woman had "attempted" marriage with a divorced man in a ceremony which was not performed by a priest. The letter, if it is authentic, offers an insight into the kind of fear which is induced by Catholic teaching. The woman has had, by her own admission, a most successful marriage of more than twenty years. She has been adored by her husband who has been patient and attentive during her illness. She has had several lovely children. Yet, with death closing in, she experiences a resurgence of the teaching of her youth. This resurgence seems to overpower her completely and she is able to write the following:

He is not really my husband. He is no more to me before God than any man who may be walking the streets tonight. . . . Now I am dying. . . . Why cannot my conscience die too? . . . What must I do to stop the torture that it inflicts on me which is so much worse than any pain caused by my disease? . . . A priest called on me once . . . he was brutal. He advised me to leave this man and do it right away. . . . I see now that all I did was tainted, that there was a curse upon my very soul. . . . Now it is too late; the chance is gone. I have made my bed . . . I must lie in it.[3]

The Protestant who would understand the great coercive power which the Roman Church can exert upon the Catholic party in an "invalid marriage" should read *Whom God Hath Not Joined*.[4] It is the story of a Roman Catholic woman who was happily married to a man of the same faith. There were several children. Eventually this woman became convinced by the teaching of her church that she was "living in sin." The reason: she had previously been married (by a priest) to another man. This marriage had lasted but briefly and was ended by divorce.

Because a priest had officiated at her first marriage, and because the man she married was still living, the woman came to believe that her present marriage (not performed by a priest) was invalid. In order to save her soul she believed she must separate from her husband. But what about the children? Finally, with the approval of the priest, she worked out with her husband's reluctant consent a plan whereby they would continue to live in the same house but would have no sexual relations. This would remove the stigma and enable them to receive the rites of the Church.

It was the threat of the rigors of hell which finally persuaded her that they must adopt the "brother and sister" arrangement. She asked herself: "Where will I be tomorrow if I am where I am today and die in my sleep?"[5] When she and her husband have elected to save their souls by living a life without sex she writes:

I thanked God . . . for awakening my false conscience . . . I often felt sorrow that I had denied Christ admittance to two souls needlessly, for so long. My very soul would shake when I thought where John and I might be now if I hadn't finally been brave and taken the stand I had felt forced to take. What if John had died while I had been dickering with God to "understand" why I had to remain in adultery?[6]

The Protestant sees in this nothing laudable, nothing devout. To him it is merely horrible. It depicts the all but incredible tyranny which a church hierarchy can exercise over one of its members. He will do well to credit it, however, for Protestants married to Roman Catholics in non-Roman rites have actually encountered it. For the Protestant, conscience is not a matter of external control but of interior conviction. For the Protestant there are no priests. There are no spiritual middlemen credentialed to mediate the divine will or to impose it upon him. But for the Roman Catholic all this is very real. His mind has been conditioned to it during childhood and youth. This to him is religion; it is the only religion he knows.

Catholic Pressures

The pressures exerted upon the Catholic living in an "invalid" marriage are deep and poignant. He must undergo a combination of mental torture, family persuasion, and social pressure. It is the tearful, reproachful look of an elderly mother. It is the heavy sigh of a sorrowing father. It is the barbed comment of a relative. It is the silent church he passes, the church whose sustaining ministries are now denied him because he is "living in sin." With all the devastation of its coercive tactics, the Roman Catholic Church can assume the posture, not of an ogre, but of a benevolent father pleading with an errant son. He or she is reminded that it is never too late to repent, that it is the Church's nature to forgive. He is constantly importuned for the good of his own soul to make peace with the Church, to end his sinful state, and to restore his hope of heaven.

There is a sum total of power in all these influences which cannot be gainsaid. The Church maintains the pressure, like drops of water falling upon stone. The state of the Roman Catholic is less difficult when he obeys his church and carries through its demand that the mixed marriage actually be a Catholic marriage in all significant respects. Even so, he encounters problems.

Francis, a young Catholic husband, reported that he had "guilt feelings" over the situation. "Of course I believe that the Catholic religion is the only true religion, and I am glad that our children are being reared in it," he said. "But I know Betty doesn't believe it, and when I see her putting up with it and co-operating with something that important that she doesn't believe in, why it seems as though it isn't quite right."

Many Catholic spouses report what they feel to be an undue pressure on them because their partner is not particularly co-operative in the matter of the religious training of the children and may exhibit latent hostility. Even when the religious agreement is being kept, the Catholic is apt to be nervous over it, wondering if the time may come when the partner will kick over the traces.

Another result reported by the Protestant partner is a feeling of complacency or superiority in the Catholic, a feeling which is sometimes communicated to the children. The Catholic spouse may tend in time to treat his wife's faith with condescension, for his parochial school textbooks have taught him that such a faith is "counterfeit." This is hard on both spouses since it poisons the entire spirit of the married relationship. Some might praise the statement we are going to quote as an example of lofty idealism. Still, one wonders just how firmly based a marriage can be when it commences as one young Catholic says he began his. "I explained very carefully to Bea that with me my religion would come first and that if there should ever develop any conflict between it and her, religion would come first— always."

Problems of the Protestant

The problems of the Protestant partner in a Protestant-Catholic marriage are more poignant than those of the Catholic. We are referring primarily to a situation where the Protestant has made the commitments which the priest demands; i.e., not to try to influence the Catholic spouse religiously and to "sign away" the children to the Catholic faith. The following letter, written by a pastor to one of his young parishioners at the request of her parents, suggests the range of the difficulties the Protestant can expect to encounter:

DEAR MARY-FRAN:

Your mother called today. She was in considerable distress over the news that you are to be married to a young man who is a Roman Catholic. She has asked me to write you and has indicated that you would be glad to hear from me. As one concerned for the happiness of both you and your prospective husband, I am happy to do so.

I am sure that your prospective husband must be a very nice guy or you would not have chosen him. He must be an estimable person in every way. Unfortunately, these are considerations which will not altogether solve or relieve the problems you will have to face because of his religion. He, your husband to be, is under a tyranny which asserts its right to invade your home and prescribe the terms on which the most intimate relationships of your marriage must be conducted. This is a blunt way to put it, but it is the truth. You have already had an introduction to this tyranny. You are to be the bride. This is your wedding. Yet you have already discovered that you will have nothing to say about the arrangements. You will have no choice of the clergyman, no choice of the church. You will have no choice in regard to any of the matters concerning the service. These arrangements have all been taken out of your hands and when you ask, "Why?" the reply is, "That's the way it has to be."

This is only a mild intimation of what lies ahead for you. This tyranny forbids you the right to witness to your own religious faith in your own home. It steps in and assumes control of your marriage and your home and will retain that control until your death. It will take from you what is precious beyond word or thought to conceive—your own dear children—and by its arbitrary decree robs you of the sacred right to guide them in spiritual matters. It forbids you to share with them the precious treasures of your own religious experience and heritage.

All this will happen not because your young man is a ruthless dictator. He may well be distressed over the situation. It will happen because he, and now you, unwittingly have become victims of this tyranny. It is this— this thing— which will outlaw you and make you a stranger in your own home. The percentage of divorce in mixed marriages is about three times as high as in marriages of the same faith. That is not surprising. What is surprising is that such marriages can ever hold together at all. Really, the only possibility of survival would be that one of the partners might become completely indifferent to his own faith. But when both are real believers, and there are children, then the situation is pretty grim. We are told so often that a marriage can succeed only when it operates on a fifty-fifty basis. In regard to religion yours is beginning on the basis of 100 to 0.

Mixed marriages sometimes survive because nature—or something more than nature—provides its own redress. The girl who signs away her children, as you are now being pressured to do, simply cannot keep the cruel and heartless bargain. As life goes on she finds it impossible to separate herself spiritually from her own flesh and blood. She may therefore permit the marriage to be broken. Or—and it is of this that I really want to speak— she may insist on the withdrawal of the old agreement made under duress and the substitution of a new agreement based on mutual love and respect. Father John A. O'Brien, noted Catholic marriage counselor, states that of every ten Catholics involved in marriage with a Protestant, six are lost to that church. This is in its way discouraging because many of these persons no doubt give up religious faith altogether. We know, however, that many of them unite with Protestant churches. It all does show that the ruthless bargain cannot be kept.

You are in love. For that reason what I say will likely have no effect on you. The trouble is that I am urging you to think. Because of your emotional engulfment it is probable that you can no longer do so. I have only this faint hope—that by a supreme effort of the will you may be able to project your mind into that future state of misery and brokenness which is indicated for you in this marriage.

One way out for you might be to accept Roman Catholicism

as your own faith. But there you are thwarted. Knowing you as well as I do, I am quite certain that you cannot go in that direction. Your background, training, and tradition—your entire life up to this point—has created a faith in you that the faith of Roman Catholicism could never displace. If you seek to embrace a faith alien to all you have ever known, you will likely come into a predicament where you find it impossible to live with yourself.

How do I know these things? How can I announce them with such apparent finality? Because, for many years now, I have listened to the anguished words of the victims of mixed marriage. Once they were where you are now—just as confident and self-assured, just as certain as you are that things would work out. They, too, were in love, with life, sweet and wonderful, before them. But the passing years, the coming of children, and all that should have deepened their joy brought them, instead, to a bitter impasse. I have been sorely distressed over the fate of these dear ones, yet there was really little or nothing to be done. There was no way that would spare grief and pain—not to one only, but to both and to the children.

Well, that's it. I've told you what a quarter of a century has taught me about the relationship you now propose to enter. Yours will be different? No: there is no difference, for this is the way it is. Saddest of all are those who try to smile and bear through gracefully while beneath the heart is hungry and alone.

One who holds you in deep affection and concern,

Facing the Commitments

One of the commitments that priests require the Protestant to make in a mixed marriage, which they control, severely curbs his or her freedom of religion. This is the pledge exacted from the Protestant that he will not do anything to interfere with the Catholic's practice of his faith. If this provision is interpreted narrowly it virtually excludes the Protestant from his faith. It must be recalled that any practice of a Protestant faith is in itself "anti-Catholic," according to theologians of that church. Also, that a basic ingredient of Protestant faith is "witness"; that is, sharing of the faith with others. Any kind of witness, either to the spouse or to the children, would be ruled out of the Catholic-controlled home on the ground of "interference."

Another commitment demanded of the Protestant, that he or she "sign away" the children to the Roman Catholic faith, is even more productive of trouble. The attempt to keep this commitment will impose impossible conditions on one of the partners. If it is the woman who is Protestant, she will be made an outsider in her own home. (It is scarcely less so in the case of a man.) She will be quite cut off from that entire vital area of the children's religious experience. She will be required to stand aloof while strangers indoctrinate her children in a faith alien to her own. She must consent to have her children taught their mother's faith is counterfeit and that it has no real right to exist. She can take this initially, but as the years pass she begins to feel intolerably lonesome and left out. She may exhibit severe emotional reactions.

Jan is a good case in point. A beautiful girl of well-to-do parents with Protestant ties which did not appear at first to be very definitively formed, Jan fell into a mixed marriage. She was much in love with handsome young Jim and signed away her children in the antenuptial agreement without any great perturbation. She was in love; nothing else mattered. One day Jan woke up to what she had done. A flash of illumination disclosed the realities of her plight. She learned that what she thought had not mattered did matter more than anything else. It appeared to her that she had lightly tossed away the one thing she really and truly cared about—her children.

The emotional shock of this experience put her in the hospital with a serious skin rash over the face and body. Her pastor who had counseled with the couple prior to their marriage was summoned to her bedside. Jan gasped out in sharp, bitter sentences the whole story of her present feelings. It was pointed out to her that she had signed the antenuptial agreement after a complete discussion of its meaning and with apparently full deliberation. Jan replied: "Of course I signed it. I would have signed anything. I was in love.

"There is just one thing wrong with that agreement," Jan went on. "You sign away children you don't have. Who can tell you what it means to have children? How can you picture to yourself or imagine what this really means? I say it can't be done. It is only when you have children that you can understand what having them means. Then I did not know; now I do know. If anybody thinks he's going to take this child from me and train her in a different faith, he's crazy. I don't care what I signed—I'm not going to do it!"

She did not do it, either. Jan had taken her stand, and she continued to stand right there. The child of Jim and Jan is not being raised Catholic; she is being raised Protestant. The marriage has survived the shock. The husband was offered a straight choice between his consent to a Protestant rearing for the child and a separation. He took the first alternative because he was deeply in love with his wife and wanted to preserve his home. The burden Jim carries is a heavy one. There are no visits back and forth with his family now. Religion kept obtruding in spite of the self-conscious efforts all around to keep the matter silent. Family occasions became unpleasant and oppressive to the point where they were finally abandoned. Things are not easy for Jim. He is cut off from his family and relatives. He has also been cut off from his church since his child is not being reared in the Catholic faith. The parish priest has used every opportunity to bring pressure to bear on him.

In a sense Jim is hoist with his own petard. He has now inherited the very fate which his church had willed for Jan. Left to their own devices, Jim and Jan could work out a satisfactory solution of their problems. But they have not been left alone, nor will they be left alone. They are beset by an "infallible" church which insists on its God-given right to train their child in religion. They are beset by parents—one set pulling against the "infallible" Church and another set pulling with it. They are caught in the middle.

It is obvious that the tensions working to tear this marriage apart are very great. The trouble here, fundamentally, is that a relationship which should embody co-operation at its finest has managed to resolve itself into a grim competition. The couple may continue to "hang together," though that is by no means certain. But it will be no better than "hanging together." There seems at this juncture to be no way out for them, no way in which the famed "give-and-take" of marriage can operate. The original ultimatum has now provoked its answering defiance, and the couple comes to an impasse in which one must apparently "win" and the other must "lose" and all concerned must suffer.

Solvitur Patiendo

The Protestant discovers that the antenuptial agreement is generally interpreted to mean complete parochial school training for all children born of the union. The Protestant, even when he does not oppose catechetical training and confirmation for the children, might desire a public school education for them. The Catholic partner might well agree to this. But the attempt to carry it out would likely incur the hostility of the parish priest.

An article in the *American Mercury* describes such a situation.[7] It is the story of a young couple who entered a mixed marriage confident that because their love was so great they would be able to "work everything out." Years later the wife said bitterly: "We worked out things by my yielding my Protestant convictions at every turn, by my being held inexorably to my signed pledge."

Once the couple did attempt on their own, in a give-and-take situation, to adjust the religious difference. The retribution of Paul's church promptly demolished the effort. The couple had agreed that their child Bob should attend parochial school up to the fourth grade, then take the latter half of his grade school work in public school so that he might have some contact with a broader type of education. The very evening of the day that their son was enrolled in the public school the priest called and belabored Paul for twenty minutes. At the end of the conversation Paul told his wife the priest had informed him that if he persisted in sending the boy to the public school, he, Paul, would be denied the sacraments of his church. The wife describes what followed:

We had a frighteningly emotional scene. I said the things I'd been storing up for twelve years. . . . I protested that I was not attempting to bring up our children outside the Catholic Church but that my pledge was now being given so rigid an interpretation that I was ready to break it. But everything Paul and I could say to each other beat helplessly against the rules his church set for the rearing of our youngsters and against the cold fact that, by digressing from those rules, he could be denied all sacraments—a sentence that would be unthinkable to him and his family. . . . I said: "We're both disregarding the promises we made to each other to 'work things out,' because we work them out only by my capitulation. . . . It's time for us to give up this marriage and separate."

They did not separate, however, though thousands of couples have separated just at that point. They managed to hang on and the marriage has survived with its heavy weight of grief and frustration for both parties.

It is not just the intrafamily relations which are likely to be impaired by religious tensions. There are wider repercussions. A host of little things which create problems for the couple may be encountered in social and business relationships. Very frequently the Protestant partner will cite the complacent and condescending attitude of Catholic friends as a disturbing circumstance. Some wives have declared that their husbands are impeded in business promotion because of a Protestant wife.

A Protestant wife, writing in a Roman Catholic publication the *Sign*, expresses some of her pent-up resentments:

My husband's work has always been in Catholic circles in various cities, and our friends and acquaintances have necessarily been drawn from his associates. I have become used to . . . being regarded with tolerance and condescension. I have found the ignorance of Protestants about Catholics fully equaled by the ignorance of Catholics regarding things Protestant, with this difference: Catholics are too smug. Feeling themselves to be members of the one true church, they have small interest in other religious groups, considering them somewhat stupid for failing to see the very obvious truths of Holy Mother Church.[3]

How Religion Dies

Religion is apt to be a casualty in a mixed marriage. It is very easy, it seems, for two faiths in one home to become no faith. All the statistical studies of mixed marriage point in that direction. This was one of the outcomes that impressed Murray H. Leiffer when he made his study of mixed marriage situations more than a decade ago.° He reports that "the first, and by far the most common (circumstance), is for one or both to completely drop out of church." He notes that of 444 men who were involved in Protestant-Catholic marriages, 110 did not have even a nominal connection with their former church and 124 had not attended church in the preceding year. Of the 449 wives (a few cases involved divorce or death of husband), sixty claimed no church affiliation and ninety-one had not attended church in the preceding year.

In some of these situations he found that religion was dropped in an effort to solve the religious problem by default. He tells of one case involving a Roman Catholic mother and a Lutheran father. Neither had attended church in years. When asked whether the religious difference had ever created any tension in the family the woman replied: "I think it is the silliest and foolishest thing in the world to argue about religion." The interviewer comments: "She and religion have made a peaceful agreement to let each other alone."

Many case studies disclose an indifferent pattern. Nat and Linda have no religious problem. Linda is a devout Catholic; Nat belongs to no church. He has no objection to the children's receiving Catholic training, even co-operates in a diffident way. He supposes it can do no harm. Yet, Nat's indifference, while it eases the situation, creates problems of its own. Bobby, the eldest, gives evidence of

following in his father's footsteps. He went through confirmation to please his mother but makes no secret of the
fact that religion has no place in his plans. He has also
formed a dislike for Father O'Hara, which complicates
things.

Statistically speaking, "solution via indifference" is the
most popular of all solutions of the mixed marriage problem. A home where tranquility is built on a calculated
ignoring of religion by one or both partners will hardly
produce devout persons. Secularists are the more likely
product.

Roman Catholic authorities, as we have seen, acknowledge that their church loses more children in mixed marriages than it keeps, despite the stipulation in the antenuptial
agreement. Protestant churches do not usually reap the
harvest, however. These children are likely candidates for
that large segment of our population—the unchurched. Too
often Protestant-Catholic marriages seem to offer either
incessant strife over religion or religious indifference. Many
partners wearily succumb to the latter. It is a way of
getting along. Hence, the paradox of mixed marriage: in
all its strife over religion, religion itself is a frequent
casualty.

Counseling in a Mixed Marriage

7

If you are contemplating marriage with a Roman Catholic, or if you are already in such a marriage with its varied problems, what sources of assistance are open to you?

Counseling may be indicated, yet wise counselors are rare. Couples undergoing the rigors of religious differences may deliberately bypass the clergy and seek out a secular counselor in order to "get away from the religious angle." The trouble is that religion is the problem and the secular counselor frequently knows little or nothing about it. That is, he may have no understanding of what religion can mean to people and hence no real grasp of the problems it can create.

Secular counselors frequently tend to interpret the religious problem in terms of emotional insecurity or inadequacy and are unable to see that it may be a problem integral to the marriage itself. Secular counselors will often suggest consultation with clergymen as resource persons. This will prove helpful.

Priest and Minister as Counselors

A Roman Catholic priest-counselor has the obvious advantage that he will assume and hold a specific position insofar as the religious differences are concerned. To this position he will urge the parties to come. His disadvantage is that he is, thus, more advocate than counselor. His position is usually known in advance to both parties so that even the appearance of an impartial arbiter is denied him. One of the partners may, presumably, have accepted the priest's position whereas the other has rejected it. This implies a kind of two-against-one situation which is not helpful for effective counseling.

The role of the priest in premarital counseling is nevertheless a useful one. In his presence the Protestant will squarely meet the full impact of the Roman Catholic position. What he has heard about Catholic demands and perhaps tended in his easygoing way to dismiss, he will now directly face. In all contemplated mixed marriages it would seem advisable for the Protestant to join his prospective spouse in conversation with a priest—provided the Catholic reciprocates in conversation with a Protestant minister. The Catholic may be refused permission to hold such a conversation. In this case the refusal is itself educational. It provides the Protestant with a good introduction to the way religious issues are handled in the Roman Catholic Church.

Even when the Catholic is forbidden to visit with the Protestant minister and feels that he must obey the order, the Protestant may wish, for his own satisfaction, to confer with the priest. Once the amenities are out of the way, the priest can be expected to present the traditional view of his church, a view which the Protestant is called upon to understand and accept.

A similar situation may develop in regard to church attendance. Each prospective partner will certainly want to attend services or masses of the other's church. This is basic to any real understanding of each other's faith. But here, as in the previous case, the couple may be frustrated by a Roman Catholic rule (Canon Law 1258) which forbids Catholics to join in worship at Protestant services. The reason for this prohibition is that Protestant worship is said to be "false worship" and a Catholic cannot attend it without "scandal." There is, of course, no corresponding barrier to Protestant attendance at a Catholic mass. A Protestant is free to attend any worship he chooses to attend. If the Catholic cannot "obtain permission" to attend a Protestant service, this fact, too, is enlightening.

The Protestant minister has certain advantages over the priest as a counselor. For one thing, he is apt to know a good deal about Roman Catholicism, whereas the priest has generally been forbidden by his church to study the nature and teaching of Protestantism. Another advantage of the minister is that he is not rigidly bound by an authoritarian church to a fixed position. Nor is he required to present an ultimatum to the couple in regard to wedding arrangements, the training of children, or the religious situation in the home. Hence, the disentanglement and fairness needed in a counselor are more likely to be found in the minister. Finally, the minister can be more effective because his concern is primarily for the couple themselves rather than for the children they may procreate. The priest is, of course, concerned for the couple, too. But his primary concern in marriage, as we have already noted, is with its progeny.

Counseling Before Marriage

The minister as counselor in situations prior to mixed marriage will serve as a source of information and suggestion. He will not pontificate but will guide and goad the couple into as thorough a confrontation of their problem as may be possible. He should know the entire area of Protestant-Catholic marriage problems very thoroughly. If he does not possess the necessary knowledge, he should acquire it. Meanwhile, he should not hesitate to refer the couple to another clergyman who may be more adequately prepared. His role is to be ready with replies to all possible questions the couples may raise. He should also be ready with the questions they should raise but do not.

The first task of the minister is to try to penetrate the deceptive halo of emotion in which the couple tends to envelop the religious problem. If he can guide them to a realistic look he will have served them well. In some cases he will fail. In some cases he will succeed and these cases will make every effort worthwhile. His task is to get the couple to see their problem, not as it is now when it is no problem, but as it will be in five years, ten years. One counselor tells of a Roman Catholic woman and a Presbyterian man who were about to marry.[1] They were asked what their plans were in regard to birth control. The woman assured the counselor that this would be no problem.

"My fiance said he wouldn't mind a dozen children," she said, "and I want four or five right away."

"What will you do after you have the fifth?" asked the counselor?

There was no answer. The counselor pointed out that the couple had merely postponed the problem till the time when they had had five children. "What a time to start an argument!," she exclaimed.

In other matters the need for realistic contemplating of the problems may be less dramatic but no less compelling. From the conversations and from the materials the minister will share with them, the couple can learn the facts about their religious dilemma. They will learn the Protestant position in regard to the nature of marriage and be able to compare it with the Roman Catholic. Sometimes a Protestant may have acquired entirely inaccurate information about Catholic teachings. He or she may be harboring some monstrous myth. In exploding this myth a skilful priest-counselor can make the position of his church appear more palatable than it really is. The Protestant minister will want to present the facts in all fairness to the Roman Church. He will also want to set forth its ultimatum on a mixed marriage in all its naked arrogance.

Attention should be given to the facts in regard to religious beliefs. What *are* the basic tenets of the faiths involved?

To answer this question, study, as well as conversation, is indicated. The couple should discuss fully and freely the differences in their faiths. They should also undertake a joint reading program which will acquaint each with the principal teachings of the other's church. The minister can make certain recommendations and the couple can also write to denominational headquarters for suggested reading.

It sometimes happens that in counseling interviews prior to a Protestant-Catholic marriage, couples give their first serious attention to what they really believe. Some astonishing results can ensue. Dean Pike tells of an Episcopalian girl and a Roman Catholic man who began to study each other's faith in preparation for marriage.[2] The study ended with the girl's becoming a Catholic and the man an Episcopalian. Then they decided they should not marry because of the incompatibility in faith!

Available Choices

A useful function of the counselor is to make clear to the

couple the different solutions which are available for their religious problem. They are thus led to see that none of the solutions may be satisfactory, that what may be open to them is a choice between something not very good and something worse. The principal possibilities can quickly be summarized:

1. Marry before a priest after meeting his full demands, each remaining in his own church but with the children to be reared Catholic.

2. Reject the Catholic ultimatum, marry before a Protestant minister, and work out the religious problem with generally agreed compromises.

3. The Protestant takes a course in Catholic doctrine and joins the Roman Catholic Church, accepting its views on marriage and other matters.

4. The Catholic studies the Protestant faith of his prospective spouse and accepts it, joining his or her church.

5. Leave the matter of the children's faith to their own choice, endeavoring to see that they have a fair introduction to both faiths.

6. Leave both churches, join a mutually acceptable third church and bring up the children in this faith.

7. Decide that the religious difference is too formidable for a successful marriage and terminate the engagement.

8. There is a further alternative which would never be considered by serious-minded persons. It is cited here only because it is the alternative into which many thousands of couples actually drift: give up any vital church connections in order to ease differences and avoid argument.

In counseling before the marriage the minister will want to have in mind fifteen "rules" which can be stated as follows:

1. Make the interview short. Do the following things: Urge a realization of the seriousness of an intra-faith obstacle; indicate the major areas of difficulty; state that there is a real possibility of working out the situation; set a date for the next meeting and suggest preparation they may wish to make.

2. Talk with both persons at the same time. Separate interviews are a waste of time, since all the ground that is covered in individual interviews must be covered again when they are together.

3. Encourage the couple to do some reading in regard to the beliefs of the respective faiths. Make specific suggestions.

4. Recommend visits with clergy of both faiths. Be ready with names of such persons in case the couple may have no active church connections. Do not hestitate to recommend a priest whom you know to be an able man.

5. Encourage discussion and the asking of questions. If you don't know the answers, say so and look them up for the next interview.

6. Ask adroit questions yourself; see to it that all necessary questions are raised.

7. Encourage the couple to articulate their differences as well as their agreements. Discourage any hiding of issues that are certain to rise later.

8. Urge the rejection of all clichés such as "Catholics never change," "Protestants must understand," "the Catholic Church is different," and so forth. Catholics frequently do change; understanding is also needed by Catholics; all churches are different or they would all be one.

9. Urge the couple to attend services in each other's church. It is important that each get the "feel" of the other's form of worship.

10. Be perfectly fair at all times. Never misrepresent the position of the Roman Catholic Church but never let it be misrepresented, either.

11. Never apologize for the Protestant position. If you think it is more fair, more democratic, more Christian than the Roman Catholic position, say so. While being meticulously fair with facts, do not hesitate to advocate Protestant views.

12. If the disparity persists and each remains firm, and if there is no immediate reason which makes their marriage advisable, strongly recommend that they not marry. Chances that such a marriage will be permanent are small.

13. If they decide to join a third church, different from the one each has previously joined, urge that such a choice should be genuine and from the heart—not a mere accommodation.

14. If one converts to the other's faith, point out the complications that can be expected and the possibility that such a conversion may not be a sincere conversion but only to ease the problem.

15. If the Protestant decides to join the Roman Church, point out that he continues to stand in the light of his conscience before God and that nothing can really change this.

Counseling After the Marriage

Many Protestant-Catholic marriages offer no overt religious problem. As we have already seen, problems may be obscured by a smog of indifference. A Protestant accepts Roman Catholic dictation, or a nominal Catholic does not bother. But when problems do become overt, what can be done about them?

In the case of a spouse, particularly the woman, who is

undergoing second thoughts about having signed the Catholic agreement, the minister-counselor will need to sound a note of encouragement. Some ministers are content to stand woodenly on the signed agreement. They wash their hands of responsibility by saying to the tortured person: "You signed it, didn't you? Now go back and keep your bargain." This approach is in its way quite as rigid as that of the priest and no more helpful.

Hope is difficult in a situation where a Protestant woman has signed away her children to a faith she cannot share. The technicalities of the situation are such as to exclude it. One must learn to look beyond them. No counselor could have helped the young mother by saying: "You made these commitments; you took these vows. It is up to you to keep them." Technically, true; but truth is always more than technicality. The person should not have gotten into the mess; but she is into it, and one must start there. The first need is a dimension of hope introduced by sympathy and understanding.

Hope must find its base in Christian faith. The tortured person must be led to realize that she is not alone in her torture. The Lord her God is with her. There is a way of deliverance, whether in the situation or out of it; and, with the help of God, that way can be found. The grace of God sufficient for any situation is sufficient also for this. Sometimes, as we have seen, the difficulties and discouragements of a Protestant-Catholic marriage drive the couple to irreligion. But the effect can be opposite. Like many other searching problems, this problem, too, can bring persons to a new dimension of faith.

The counselor knows that there is hope not only in God but in people. Many situations which appear to be altogether rigid are not really so. Minds can change, people can change. All human situations are really mobile and, being mobile, are subject to change. The fact of potential, or possibility, in any human situation must not be overlooked. The virtue of patience, to which a mixed marriage is itself conducive, can produce amazing changes in apparently hopeless situations. The best instrument of change is the person who, steadfast but not rigid, shows forth the spirit of Christ in daily relationships.

Situation Mobile

✓ A prime responsibility of the counselor is to let the couple see that their situation is not permanently fixed. If religious positions have hardened into inflexibility and neither partner can think of the situation as fluid and subject to adjustment, any modus vivendi becomes extremely difficult. In a case where the Protestant partner has become disturbed over the effects of the Catholic antenuptial agreement, achievement of mobility becomes essential.

The Catholic partner often uses the signed statement as a weapon in developing a cold war. "You signed it," he will say, "I believed you were acting in good faith. Why do you go back on your word?"

This is all true enough but not very helpful. The fact is that the Roman Catholic agreement when enforced upon a devout Protestant mother is an agreement "against nature." We have examined some of its effects in chapter 6. The early training of children in religion is as natural as eating. It is elemental for a mother's thought of God to flow to her child in the intimacy of the early years. At this point, mother and child are one. The Roman Catholic agreement would disrupt this experience at its most significant point. Since her religion is regarded as false, she is forbidden to share it with her child. Spiritual dictators have decreed that at the point of religion the natural rapport between mother and child must be broken, or rather, never permitted to form.

The mental anguish of a mother forced to live under such conditions is unspeakable and frequently unbearable. She is doomed to watch a chasm between her and her child steadily widen and deepen. When there can be no intimacy in things that are dearest and deepest, alienation may grow in other ways. The mother may react in resentment against the Church which thus intrudes upon her home. The result may be a growing bitterness against her husband who lacks the courage to stand against his church. Neurotic behavior and physical illness are not uncommon. The woman is being required to violate her own nature and the strain may be too great.

The case of the Protestant father who has signed the agreement may be quite as tragic. The reaction may be slower in his case but it is no less certain. As the years pass and his children grow to maturity, he is beset with a growing sense of loneliness. He sees his wife and children participating in events from which he is spiritually excluded. He realizes increasingly that he is alone. Between him and those dearest to him there is a fixed gulf. His is a life of quiet frustration in a Roman Catholic household which tolerates but does not include him.

Such are the problems for which relief is sought. To cite the agreement signed under the duress of romance as the "solution" of these problems is to be unrealistic. This is like Shylock's insisting on his pound of flesh according to the contract. A marriage cannot be successfully built on such a basis. The Catholic party may even find it necessary to develop some "give-and-take" on an issue which he had assumed to be closed.

Once the agreement has been signed, it is certainly a factor in any subsequent situation. But it is only one factor among others. Another factor may be the health of the mother who has found it impossible to live with the agreement. The mother may find herself in this painful dilemma: the agreement which love induced her to sign, conscience now bids her repudiate. The emotional conflict at this point may become so serious that relief of some kind is imperative. If something is not worked out to ease the tension, the marriage itself may be jeopardized.

If the couple can agree to take a wholly new look at their problem and to seek new approaches to its solution, there can be hope in even the most deadlocked situation. Without this openness of view the marriage may have to terminate. The marriage can survive at this point only by the determination of two devoted persons who will take matters into their own hands, resolutely reject outside interference, and work out their own problem in their own way. The gravest difficulty is that this solution involves more maturity and restraint than most human beings possess.

Live Options

Counseling in mixed marriage is, in part, the art of introducing the couple to the possible. If there are certain things that just cannot be done, there may be other things that could be done. It is the counseling task to discover what these possibilities are and to explore them with the couple. Here are some guides that may be helpful both to counselors and those seeking counsel.

1. Frankly face and discuss the religious difference when appropriate to do so. Do not try to hide it or to pretend it is not there.

2. Recognize that previous agreements, while entered into in good faith, may be subject to change.

3. List the things that could be done in regard to the religious situation. Note possibilities of agreement and concessions that each might be willing to make.

4. Appraise the possibilities of conversion of each to the other's faith. If there seems to be no chance of this, either way, agree to terminate or set reasonable limits to such efforts.

5. Be imaginative, be willing to contemplate solutions which may not have previously occurred.

6. Appraise the family and church pressures which are working against the marriage and devise strategies in regard to them.

7. Neither talk down nor unduly tout your own religion. Do the best possible thing with it—live it.

8. Recognize that the preservation of the home is a value in itself and worth substantial concessions on both sides.

Once the live option idea has gained acceptance, the active exploration of possibilities can commence. None of these "solutions" is completely satisfactory. There is no such solution available. Yet devout and devoted couples have been able to preserve their home in spite of acute religious differences. Dick and Portia have maintained their home on the basis of "individual choice" so far as religious faith is concerned. At twelve years of age the children were given instruction in both faiths—Roman Catholic (the father) and Presbyterian (the mother). Then, on the basis of personal choice, the child became either a Roman Catholic or a Presbyterian.

The difficulty here is in maintaining the even balance which such an agreement implies. In the above instance both children became Presbyterians. Is it not possible that the mother unconsciously slanted the children's thinking? If she did so, could she be accused of being "unfair"? Is it not a mother's function to "slant" her children's thinking in this fashion? If this were so, was not the father, in his way, also seeking to "slant" their thinking in another direction. If so, would he be censored for doing what a father ought to be doing? The problems here, as in any "solution," are immense. The point is that the solution "worked" in this situation. Four lives are together in a reasonably satisfactory arrangement and a family unit has been preserved in integrity.

Pat and Muriel found their formula in simple alternation. Sig, the oldest, went to parochial school and into the Roman Catholic faith. Patricia went to public school and the Methodist church. Then Betsy to the Catholic and Arthur to the Methodist. But this calculated impartiality did not work out. Sig has been going over to the Methodist church with Arthur, likes it and is talking of becoming a Methodist minister. Betsy has been going with friends to the Catholic Church, likes it better and wants to become a Catholic.

Francis and Marjorie were married by a priest after making the commitments which he demanded. They have worked it out between themselves, however, to send the children to public schools and to alternate by years in the matter of religious training. One year they attend services and classes at the Congregational church with their mother. Next year they go to mass and to catechism with their father. When they have attained sufficient maturity they will make their own decision. The mother remarks on the situation in language which is in itself revealing: "I can see how it's going to work out now. Barbara will be a Catholic. I can tell because she's so superstitious!"

The advantage of some such arrangement is its freedom.

It leaves a little elbow room, a little space created by patience and restraint in which personalities can breathe. The role of the parents is extremely difficult. They must avoid vacuous tolerance on the one hand, and rigorous conversionism on the other. The hazards are obvious, but the alternative may be a broken home.

Premarital and Postmarital Counseling

There is a possible connection which sometimes develops between premarital and postmarital counseling in Protestant-Catholic marriage. It is worth comment. Any minister who has been at all active in marriage counseling has had the experience of seeing couples with whom he counseled prior to their marriage return to him for further counseling at a later date. It is no satisfaction to him to note that the marriage has begun to founder on the very rocks he so painstakingly charted for the couple during the previous visits.

Floyd said: "We have come back because you knew what you were talking about. You tried to help us before. Now will you try to help us again?"

In one sense the situation has improved. The veil of emotionalism has been withdrawn and the couple are now ready to face what they would not face before. The possibilities of solution have constricted; there is less room for maneuver. But there is now a will to seek a solution and this is essential. Such a circumstance does point up the value of premarital counseling in Protestant-Catholic marriages, even when it appears to fail in the immediate context. While there may seem to be no positive result at the time and the couple plunge unthinkingly into a marriage replete with problems they refuse to acknowledge, there may be lasting benefits. The couple may at least be equipped with some background of understanding for the religious problem. They may in time begin to evaluate the problems they so lightly brushed aside during the premarital conversations. In this case the previous counseling will prove a distinct advantage.

Mixed Marriages
and the Law

8

The legal problems of a Protestant-Catholic marriage are certainly not the first concern of Christian partners. There may well come a moment in the marriage, however, when the matter of one's legal rights becomes of great interest. This may be particularly true of persons who have signed the Roman Catholic antenuptial agreement. What is the legal status of the agreement?

Church and State Control of Marriage

It will be useful before answering this question to review the question of the relation of church to state in the matter of authority over marriage. We have already touched on this topic in chapter two.

Protestants have agreed that marriage, while of solemn, spiritual significance, is not a sacrament of the church and that it is a matter of civil as well as of religious concern. Generally, they have been content to leave the field of legislation regarding marriage and divorce to the state, while maintaining a moral interest to see that such legislation did not violate God's law. The Roman Catholic Church has held, to the contrary, that marriage is one of the seven sacraments of the Church. As such, its control should be in the hands of the one true Church, the Roman Catholic.

Catholic leaders recognized that the state also had an interest in the marriage of citizens. The civil effects of marriage, were, of course, a matter for the state. In the basic marriage law of the Roman Church, Canon 1016, it should be recognized that the word "church" as used here refers to the Roman Catholic Church, and that the authority of this church is presumed to extend over all Christians. Canon 1016 draws this comment from Father Joseph P. O'Brien:

Marriage contracted between baptized persons is a social contract that works for the public good of the society that is the Church. . . . The authority which alone can exercise jurisdiction over such marriages is the Church. . . . The Church, then, has the power of legislating all things for the valid and licit marriage of Christians. . . .[1]

In certain countries where it is able to exercise political influence the Roman Catholic Church has, by means of a concordat, included its control of the marriage of baptized persons in the country's laws. So the concordat between Colombia and the Vatican provides:

Article 17. Marriage undertaken by all those who profess the Catholic religion will produce civil effects with respect to the persons and property of the spouses and their children only when it is performed according to the dispositions of the Council of Trent. . . .

Article 18. Regarding marriages performed at any time . . . the supplementary proofs of ecclesiastical origin have the preference.

Article 19. Only the ecclesiastical authority has the exclusive prerogative to determine the marriage causes (reasons) that may affect the marriage union and the cohabitation of the spouses, as well as anything relative to the validity of the engagement. . . .

In Spain, a country where Roman Catholic influence is compulsively strong, religious discrimination against Protestants has been written into law—the Charter of the Spanish People, 1945, and the Concordat between Spain and the Vatican, 1953. The key provision in the former document states: "In the matter of acknowledgment of a mixed marriage between Catholic and non-Catholic persons, the state shall formulate its legislation so as to harmonize with Canon Law."

There is provision in Spanish law for a civil marriage for non-Christians, that is, for those who have not been baptized. But this is little help to Protestants. Many of them were baptized Catholic in infancy. From this mark of Catholicism there is virtually no escape. The person who seeks civil marriage must "prove" that he is not a Catholic to the satisfaction of a local cleric. At best, this can be achieved only after interminable delay and, generally, not at all. This means in practice that Protestants desiring to be legally married in Spain are placed in the impossible position of having to go to a priest for the ceremony. Protestant marriage rites have no legal effects in Spain.

Dr. Piper feels that this domination of marriage arrangements by the Roman Catholic Church poses a moral issue for Protestants. He is sure that no Protestant couple could submit to a marriage ceremony on such terms. He asserts that the Protestant is justified in foregoing public acknowledgment of his marriage, "even at the risk of casting the slur of illegitimacy upon his children."[2] This problem is much more than academic in Spain where many Protestant couples have had to confront it.

One Spanish Protestant couple, after trying many times to obtain permission for a civil marriage, were married in a Protestant ceremony. They then listed themselves as married on the civil register of Madrid. The man, Antonio Mendez Morlans, was brought to trial in 1959 for the "crime" of stating falsely that he and his wife were married. Antonio Mendez Morlans was acquitted on technicalities, but the court dared not raise the slightest question about the right of the Roman Catholic Church to impose its canon law on Protestants. This is a basic law of Spain.

In the United States the Roman Catholic Church has never been able to achieve enforcement of its denominational marriage rules in civil law. Its clergy have, however, sought to influence their parishioners, including lawyers and judges, in regard to their handling of such matters as divorce cases. We have already noted a diocesean rule requiring Catholic lawyers to "clear" divorce cases with the local bishop before proceeding in court. This represents an attempt to impose the traditional Roman Catholic control on American jurisprudence.

Roman Catholic leaders have also sought to influence the performance of Catholic judges on this and other church-state matters by means of a Catholic code of professional ethics.[3] The object is to induce Roman Catholic laymen to follow canon law rather than American civil law in divorce and adoption procedures. The Roman Catholic Church has waged an unrelenting struggle to secure status as an enforceable contract in law for the antenuptial agreement which it requires in mixed marriages. To date, this struggle has had little success, but it continues.

One of the favorite legislative goals of the Roman

Catholic hierarchy is a law governing religious practice in adoption procedures. This law would require courts and adoption agencies to choose foster parents or institutions of the same religion as the natural parents. Catholic leadership has succeeded in obtaining some such law in a number of states. In Massachusetts the law provides that in making orders for adoption the judge shall "when practicable" give custody only to persons of the same faith as that of the child. The law also contains a stipulation that if the court does award custody to persons of another faith, "the court shall state the facts which impelled it to make such a disposition."

Most such laws do contain a saving qualification such as "when practicable" or "shall be preferred." Yet, if narrowly construed, these laws can be compulsive in application. The Roman Church has been known to press for such literal enforcement that it would tear a child from a happy home and loving parents in order to place her in a Catholic orphanage, thus assuring her a Catholic education. For example, in the Hildy Ellis case, the Catholic press could and did argue that the Church was only seeking to uphold law and order.

Will the Antenuptial Agreement Hold in Court?

Those who inquire as to whether courts will enforce the Catholic antenuptial agreement as a legal contract may be advised that generally they will not. The agreement is not a legally binding contract which courts will compel a person to observe. The matter is usually viewed as spiritual in nature—like the vow to "honor and obey" which is contained in many ceremonies. Such commitments have their significance but they are not in the nature of contracts enforceable by law. The preponderance of American case law follows this line. There are, to be sure, a few decisions which apparently differ, but these are exceptions which only indicate the rule. Legally speaking, a Protestant is not obligated to keep a Roman Catholic antenuptial agreement.

There are several compelling reasons why the courts have taken this position. One reason is the First Amendment, which bars laws "respecting an establishment of religion or prohibiting the free exercise thereof." Under this limitation, courts have felt unable to assume the prerogative of choosing the "right" religion for parties in their jurisdiction. So a court held: "Under the Constitution . . . the law may not profess to know what is a right belief. It may control the religious upbringing only to the extent necessary to protect temporal welfare."[4]

The Massachusetts court declared that "the court will not itself prefer one church to another."[5] The United States Supreme Court has declared that "the law knows no heresy and is committed to the support of no dogma."[6] One church-state authority went so far as to describe avoidance of official involvement with religion in these terms:

A judge convinced that a child will die if it does not receive an immediate blood transfusion can constitutionally direct the giving of the transfusion over the parent's objection. A judge equally convinced that the parent's refusal to baptize his dying child will deprive the child of eternal salvation is constitutionally without power to take any legal action.[7]

Welfare of the Child

Courts are not concerned to arbitrate and choose among religions in cases involving custody. They have chosen a different criterion for their decisions—the temporal welfare of the child. This is a second reason for refusal to enforce the antenuptial agreement as a legal contract. In child custody cases the court decides, not on the basis of a religious agreement, but on the basis of what seems best for the child's welfare. To put it another way, if an antenuptial agreement is being violated and the child in question is thriving in spite of it, then it is too bad for the agreement. The court will not disturb a child in order to enforce the agreement. Dr. Pfeffer even raises the question as to whether a deceased parent himself would want it otherwise: "It is a questionable presumption that a deceased parent would have chosen religious continuity rather than temporal happiness and welfare for his child."[8]

In a 1961 case, the Pennsylvania Supreme Court refused the plea of a natural father to regain direction of his son's religious training. The son of Mr. and Mrs. Charles Bendrick had been baptized Catholic. During a period of estrangement from her husband, Mrs. Bendrick placed the child, still an infant, in the custody of Belvey C. White, a Protestant minister, and his wife. The Bendricks were later divorced. Thereupon Mr. Bendrick brought suit to regain custody in order that the child might be reared Catholic. On the basis of the welfare of the child, the Supreme Court sustained a lower court in awarding custody to the Whites. Justice Benjamin R. Jones said for the court:

Proper religious training of a child is most important and a factor which must be given the most serious consideration. However, such a factor, while of great weight, is not controlling.

As a general rule courts should endeavor to place the custody of a child with persons of the same religious faith. But bearing in mind the paramount importance of the general welfare of the child, courts may, in the exercise of sound discretion, place the child in the custody of persons of a different religious faith if the child's welfare so demands.[9]

This Pennsylvania case is of particular interest because of a Pennsylvania law which states that "persons of the same religious persuasion as the parents of the minors shall in all cases be preferred by the court in their appointment as guardians of the persons of such minors."

In the Massachusetts case the court declared unequivocally: "If (the wishes of the parents) as to the religious training and surroundings of the children cannot be carried into effect without sacrificing what the court sees to be for the welfare of the child, they must so far be disregarded."[10]

In a Missouri case the court was confronted with a habeas corpus instituted by a Catholic father to secure custody of his child whose mother was dead. The child had been placed for adoption with a Protestant couple. The court refused to disturb the child on the ground that she had made a satisfactory adjustment in her home.[11]

States which have a law that instructs authorities to place children only where they can receive religious training in the faith of the natural parent, often present a grave problem in custody cases. Even here, however, courts have often taken advantage, where needed, of the qualifying phrase which is usually present in such laws. The Massachusetts law contains the phrase "when practicable." Massachusetts courts have humanely used this loophole in a number of cases. In the Gally case, 1952, for example, the Supreme Court overruled a probate judge who had refused to approve the adoption by Protestant foster parents of a two-year-old child born to Roman Catholic parents.[12] The natural mother stated for the record that she had no objection to the change in the child's religion. The report on the home and the ability of the couple to care adequately for the child was excellent. The Supreme Court held that the "when practicable" phrase empowered it to exercise discretion and declared that "in view of all these circumstances it would not be 'practicable' in this instance to 'give custody only to persons of the same religious faith as that of the child.' "[13]

It is significant that the Boston *Pilot*, an extreme Catholic publication which is the official organ of the Boston archdiocese, savagely attacked the Gally decision and like decisions since. The paper referred to the Gally decision as a "supreme tragedy" and "a victory for the current secularist philosophy."[14]

Even in a situation where there has been a postnuptial agreement between the parties in regard to the religious training of a child, the court will generally refuse to enforce it against what seems to be the child's temporal welfare. In *Martin* vs. *Martin,* the New York Court of Appeals disregarded such an agreement, even though it had been signed by both parties in a divorce decree. The court held that the child's present welfare required deletion from the decree of the provision for Catholic religious training.[15]

The welfare of the child is the court's general criterion in the determination of custody, and the criterion is applied alike in situations where the Catholic party has died, where the couple are separated and one has custody, and where foster parents have custody with the parents either living or dead. In his thorough discussion of the question of religious training in the upbringing of children, Dr. Leo Pfeffer calls attention to an unequivocal statement in an article already noted:

No mere agreement as to the religious education of children between father and mother, before or after marriage, is binding and it is always open to either parent to change his mind, as it is his privilege to inculcate upon his children these religious principles which for the time being seem best to him.[16]

There is a conflict at this point between American courts and the Roman Catholic Church. The latter subordinates the interests of the couple and the family to its own denominational interest. In custody issues it pursues the same course, frankly subordinating the temporal welfare of the child to "eternal welfare considerations"; that is, to the matter of training in Roman Catholic theology.

Freedom of Religion

A third reason for unenforceability of the Catholic antenuptial agreement is that it interferes with freedom of religion. One of the basic religious rights is that of choosing the religion one prefers. Integrally related to this and, indeed, a part of it, is the right to choose the faith in which one's child is to be reared. Just as it would be contrary to freedom to abridge a person's right to change his own religious practices, so it would be contrary to freedom to abridge this right in regard to his children. For this reason, courts usually will not enforce a contract not to change the religious upbringing of one's children. This is particularly true in states (Colorado and Ohio are examples) where guarantees of such freedom are specifically set forth.

In any conflict between an antenuptial agreement and the present desire of the parent the agreement must give way.

A famous Missouri case *Brewer* vs. *Cary* is frequently cited for its clear enunciation of this principle.[17] In this case the court decided that the surviving parent is the normal guardian for minor children and that he or she should possess full right to choose the child's religious training. This should be the case, despite any challenge on this point by godparents or collateral relatives. Any attempt to assign co-guardianship to specific parents (such as godparents, for example) is not comparable to the assignment of property

action by collateral relatives, godparents, or even by one of the natural parents, on behalf of an antenuptial agreement, is apt to be rebuffed. Neither the recorded wishes of a dead parent nor the declaration of a living, natural parent can, as a rule, disturb a surviving parent or legal guardian in the exercise of this right of choice.[22]

Difficulties in Practice

Still another reason for refusal of the courts to enforce the antenuptial agreement is the impracticability of any effort to do so. There are almost insuperable difficulties in enforcement, even in situations where both spouses are living.[23] Theoretically it would be possible for a court to compel the Protestant in certain specific observances such as baptism. But the Protestant (or Catholic if he had agreed to a Protestant stipulation) could hardly be suppressed in the expression of his personal religious views. Nor would there be any ready way to deter him or her from nullifying the formal religious training of the child by contrary instruction in private. A court is likely to find this matter most elusive of its decrees.

Imagine the status of a parent under court order to bring up his child in a faith which he has come to detest. What kind of religious training could be expected from one who believed that the religion enforced would assure eternal damnation of the child? Where religion is concerned the heart is foremost. If the heart is not in it the entire effort is suspect. Surely, as they planned their marriage, the parties had no thought of a legally-binding contract when they made their agreement. Neither thought in terms of his ability to hale the other into court should there be a subsequent difference of opinion. It is impracticable, and possibly cruel as well, to disrupt child-care arrangements merely to satisfy a denominational demand. As a rule, courts will not do so.

Contrary Decisions

The general direction of the courts is clear: they have refused to enforce the Roman Catholic antenuptial agreement. We have noted, however, that there were some contrary decisions. In *Begley* vs. *Begley* the courts first sustained, then were noncommittal in regard to the agreement.[24] Mr. Begley, a Roman Catholic, sought a separation. He also sought custody of the children on the ground that Mrs. Begley, contrary to the antenuptial agreement, was rearing them in the Protestant faith.

Mrs. Begley, a Protestant, had signed the Roman Catholic agreement prior to marriage. She contended that she had been coerced by her fiancé into signing the agreement. Circumstances made the marriage desirable and her fiancé threatened to leave her if she would not sign. Mrs. Begley contended further that as an individual she had, in separation, the right to decide the question of her children's religious training. She stated that under no circumstances would she bring up her children as Roman Catholics. "I will die rather than yield," she said.

Justice Charles J. Beckinella granted Mr. Begley a separation and also gave him custody of the children. He declared the Catholic antenuptial agreement to be "valid and enforceable" and noted that "the infants by baptism have been initiated into the Catholic faith. They should be permitted to continue in that faith without interference until such time as they are old enough to make a choice of their own." It appeared that Justice Beckinella had made the Catholic rite of baptism rather than the decision of the parent the controlling factor.

The Court of Appeals reversed Justice Beckinella, basing its decision solely on the welfare of the children. The justices stated that in their opinion the welfare of the children, aged two to five, would be better served if they remained with their mother. As to the enforceability of the antenuptial agreement, however, the court remained carefully non-committal. The justices said:

In reaching this decision we do not pass upon the enforceability of the prenuptial agreement. The question may be presented at a later time when the children have reached the age which makes them less dependent upon mother care and which gives them sufficient maturity to receive religious instruction.

At least one instance can be offered in which the New York courts unequivocally sustained the desire of a natural mother in regard to the religious training of children, even though this meant interference with the children's status and possible harmful effects upon them.[25] Two little girls baptized Catholic in infancy were assigned to a Jewish couple and became well adjusted in this home. The natural mother disappeared and nothing was heard from her for a considerable time. When the Jewish couple sought to adopt the children the mother reappeared, asserting that she wanted them reared Catholic. The lower court denied her petition on the ground that she had no real interest in the religious training of the children. The court found that while they had been baptized Catholic, the Protestant father had never consented to this; also that the children had found in the Jewish home happiness, love, and security, and that to remove them would be harmful.

In question was the interpretation of the New York law which provides that a child assignment "must be made, when practicable," to an agency "under the control of persons of the same religious faith and persuasion as that of the child." The law even provides that the court "may at any time during the progress of the proceedings . . . vacate any commitments previously made when it is shown to the satisfaction of the court that a mistake was made in adjudicating the child's religion." On the basis of these provisions, the Court of Appeals reversed the lower court, declaring that the reversal was mandatory under the statute. Dr. Pfeffer contends that "only by assuming the irrevocability of infant baptism until the age of reason and discretion can the Santos decision be adequately explained."[26]

There are other cases which seem to favor enforceability of the Roman Catholic agreement. Perhaps the most notable, though it is a decision of a lower court only, is that in the New York case of *Ramon* vs. *Ramon*.[27] In his decision, Justice O'Brien sustained the Catholic antenuptial agreement and ordered resumption of the child's training in a Catholic boarding school. The language of the court indicates high deference to the canon law of the Roman Catholic Church which is copiously quoted along with the pronouncements of Pope Pius XI and other Catholic dignitaries. "It is important to note," the judge remarked, "that it was only by a concurrence of these obligations (he referred primarily to Catholic training of the child) that the respondent's membership in the Catholic Church would be assured and continued."

"The law favors antenuptial agreements," Justice O'Brien went on to say, "and they will be enforced according to the intention of the parties." In his decision he relied heavily on *Weinberger* vs. *Van Hessen* and quotes from it this statement: "Agreements between parties for a particular sect of religious upbringing have in general been valid in this country."[28] The Weinberger case concerned a suit brought against a person who had promised to support a child if he could direct his religious upbringing. In this specific performance instance, the court sustained the agreement and required him to pay. In his discussion of the Weinberger case, Dr. Pfeffer points to the curious fact that the cases on which the Court of Appeals based its decision had actually been decided on the opposite basis, the court in each instance having refused to enforce an agreement regarding religious training against what it deemed to be the welfare of the child.[29]

It is worth note that most of the decisions enforcing the Catholic agreement have been in the New York court. Many lawyers believe that the recent decision in *Martin* vs. *Martin* has probably overruled prior decisions in this state.[30] In the latter case the Court of Appeals disregarded a Catholic antenuptial agreement which it averred would be harmful to the child if enforced.

The Moral Concern

For the Christian the problem of the Catholic agreement must be considered in another dimension. What is required of a person who endeavors to be true to his conscience? Suppose a person who has signed the Catholic antenuptial agreement becomes convinced that its terms are immoral and violate conscience. What if he arrives at the conviction that it is morally wrong for him (or her) to maintain the terms of the agreement? The answer that one is in honor bound to keep his word does not quite cover the moral ambiguities of this predicament.

While it would be a point difficult to establish legally, there is certainly a measure of duress involved in every Roman Catholic agreement signed by a Protestant. Sometimes the duress is overt, as in the case of a Protestant who is under pressure to marry in order to protect an unborn child. A Roman Catholic man may decline consent to the ceremony until the Catholic ultimatum has been accepted. Far more often it is the simple coercion of love. When a Protestant woman has become emotionally committed to a Catholic man, a calm and careful appraisal of the Catholic wedding terms is an impossibility. Such consideration as is given to the Catholic demands is cursory and brief. There is no real confrontation of the issues. That is to come later, and it generally comes.

The Protestant, already bent on marriage with the Catholic, is apt to regard the agreement as merely another stone in the road. It is something to get over or around so that the wedding can take place. The man and woman are under the influence of the potent narcotic of love. Is there something to be signed? Just hand them the pen! Sign it? Of course they will sign! They will sign anything because they are in love. This is an agreement signed under emotional pressure and duress. There comes a day when this duress is no longer felt in the same way. Other factors —one's faith, one's children—have now entered the picture.

Is there, then, virtue in maintaining commitments which outrage one's deepest nature? Is there virtue in living the lie of compliance with clerical demands? Or has the time come, rather, for a new look at the entire matter? When that day comes there is no perfect solution for what has the aspect of an impossible problem. But this much the couple can do and this much they ought in Christian conscience to do: they should, first, disregard clerical dictation. Counsel and suggestion they need and should welcome, but dictation from outsiders is simply irrelevant. Let these two—and no others—frankly face the problem which is uniquely their own. Let them look at it frankly and clear-eyed and let them arrive at their own solution. This is a hard thing. Some say it is impossible. But there is one thing that is more impossible—the effort to stand slavishly upon an agreement that is undemocratic, un-American, un-Christian, and coercive from the first.

Notes

Chapter 1

1. *Religious News Service* (New York), December 27, 1957.

2. See John T. Landis, "Marriage of Mixed and Non-Mixed Religious Faith," *American Sociological Review,* June, 1949, pp. 401-07.

3. See *op. cit.,* pp. 401-09.

4. The *Tablet* (Brooklyn), January 11, 1958.

5. *Information* (New York), February, 1954, p. 34.

6. Bishops' Committee on Mixed Marriage, *A Factual Study of Mixed Marriage,* National Catholic Welfare Conference, Washington, D. C., 1943.

7. The *Register* (Denver), November 25, 1956.

8. D. R. Mace, "The Truth About Mixed Marriages," *Woman's Home Companion,* July, 1951.

9. Article in *American Ecclesiastical Review,* January, 1946.

10. The *Tablet,* April 19, 1958.

11. *New York Times,* March 15, 1956.

12. *Washington Post,* January 4, 1958.

13. "Religious News Service," (New York), February 5, 1960.

14. *Op. cit.*

15. *Ave Maria* (Notre Dame), November 24, 1956.

16. The *Voice of St. Jude* (Chicago), June, 1957.

17. *New York Herald Tribune,* March 22, 1959.

Chapter 2

1. The most complete presentation of the Roman Catholic view is in Pope Pius XI, *Encyclical on Christian Marriage,* December 31, 1930. See the translation by Gerald C. Treacy, S. J., New York, Paulist Press.

2. These quotations are from the translation by T. L. Bouscaren and A. C. Ellis, *Canon Law: a Text and Commentary* (Milwaukee: The Bruce Publishing Co., 1951 and 1957).

3. Bishop John F. Deardon, as quoted in *Church and State* (Washington), September, 1958, p. 8.

4. The *Catholic Register* (Denver), July 6, 1958.

5. *National Catholic Almanac* (Paterson, New Jersey: St. Anthony's Guild, 1948), p. 231.

6. *Church and State,* February, 1958; *New York Times,* February 27, 1958.

7. *New York Times,* March 4, 1958.

8. *Our Sunday Visitor* (Huntington, Ind.), August 25, 1957. See also the *Catholic Review* (Baltimore), September 17, 1949.

9. The *Tablet,* August 31, 1957.

10. *Ibid.,* March 1, 1958.

11. *Ibid,* April 23, 1955.

12. For a discussion of this point see George Hayward Joyce, *Christian Marriage* (New York: Sheed & Ward Inc., 1933), pp. 208-09.

13. *New York Times,* June 20, 1958; *Time,* July 7, 1958.

14. The *Pilot* (Boston), April 17, 1948.

15. The entire exchange is printed in the parish publication *St. Edmund's Advocate* (Wheeling, W. Va.), April, 1959.

16. John A. O'Brien, *The Truth About Mixed Marriages* (Huntington, Ind.: Our Sunday Visitor Press, 1953), p. 50.

17. The *Sign* (Union City, New Jersey), April, 1959.

18. *Our Sunday Visitor,* February 14, 1960.

19. Msgr. Francis J. Connell in *American Ecclesiastical Review* (Washington), October, 1959.

20. The *Pilot,* June 18, 1960.

21. Diemer vs. Diemer, 391 N. Y. (App. 1960); also *New York Law Journal,* June 24, 1958 and October 10, 1960.

22. *Church and State,* May and July, 1957. The case was widely publicized by the nation's press during this period.

23. The *Tablet,* June 19, 1954.

Chapter 3

1. Charles R. Bell, Jr., "Don't Sign with Your Fingers Crossed!" *Christian Century,* LXX (1953), 447.

2. Warren C. Lilly, S.J., "Mixed Marriages," *ibid.,* 548.

3. Winfred E. Garrison, *A Protestant Manifesto* (New York: Abingdon Press, 1952), pp. 144-45.

4. See Roland H. Bainton, *What Christianity Says About Sex, Love and Marriage* (New York: Association Press, 1957), pp. 76-77.

5. The Lambeth Report (1958), section V, reprinted in Richard M. Fagley, *The Population Explosion and Christian Responsibility* (New York: Oxford University Press, 1960, pp. 229-30.

6. Quoted in *ibid.,* pp. 198-99.

7. Norman Vincent Peale, "Answers . . . ," *Look,* March 22, 1955.

8. The *Tablet,* March 26, 1955.

Chapter 4

1. Daniel A. Lord, *Questions I'm Asked About Marriage* (St. Louis: The Queen's Work, Inc., 1938), p. 41.

2. The *Register,* February 6, 1949.

3. *Time,* November 4, 1946.

4. *Christian Heritage* (See Cliff, New York), June, 1946. Formerly *The Converted Catholic.*)

5. 98 U.S. 145 (1878).

6. 133 U.S. 333 (1890).

7. *New York Times,* March 3, 1932.

8. Proclaimed by the pope in *Ne Temere* (1908) and in the new canon law promulgated in 1917. (Unfortunately the new law does not appear to have been retroactive.)

9. Reinhold Niebuhr, *The Children of Light and the Children of Darkness* (New York: Charles Scribner's Sons, 1944), p. 151.

Chapter 5

1. Pope Pius XI, *op. cit.*

2. The bishop's statement was featured widely in the press. For the full text see the *New York Times*, November 28, 1959.

3. In an address to the Planned Parenthood Federation of Chicago, reported in the *Churchman* (St. Petersburg, Fla.), November 1, 1947.

4. Paul Blanshard gives a detailed account of the point on Onan in his *American Freedom and Catholic Power* (Boston: The Beacon Press, 1958), pp. 167 f.

5. E. C. Blake and G. B. Oxnam, "A Protestant View of a Catholic for President," *Look*, May 10, 1960, p. 33.

6. George A. Kelly, *The Catholic Marriage Manual*, Imprimatur Cardinal Spellman (New York: Random House Inc., 1958), pp. 46-47.

7. Fagley, *op. cit.*, p. 189.

8. The full text appeared in the *New York Times*, February 24, 1961.

9. Otto A. Piper, *The Biblical View of Sex and Marriage* (New York: Charles Scribner's Sons, 1960), p. 146.

10. As this is being written the case has again gone to the Supreme Court.

11. *New York Times*, June 22, 1960.

12. For a full discussion of the Roman Catholic view, see Edwin F. Healy, S.J., *Medical Ethics*, Imprimatur Cardinal Stritch (Chicago: Loyola University Press, 1956).

13. See Donald T. Mather, *Liguorian* (Liguori, Mo.), July, 1955.

Chapter 6

1. *Information* (New York), November, 1951.
2. *Tidings* (Los Angeles), August 15, 1958.
3. *Liguorian,* June, 1953.
4. Claire McAuley, *Whom God Hath Not Joined* (New York: Sheed & Ward Inc., 1961).
5. *Ibid.,* p. 36.
6. *Ibid.,* p. 135.
7. *American Mercury* (New York), January, 1950.
8. The *Sign,* February, 1952.
9. See especially Murray H. Leiffer, "Mixed Marriages and Church Loyalties," *Christian Century,* January 19, 1949.

Chapter 7

1. Norman M. Lobsenz, "How Successful Are Inter-Faith Marriages?" *Redbook* (New York), October, 1956.
2. James A. Pike, *If You Marry Outside Your Faith* (New York: Harper & Brothers, 1954), p. 176.

Chapter 8

1. Joseph P. O'Brien, *Right of the State to Make Disease an Impediment to Marriage* ("Catholic University of America Studies in Sacred Theology, Second Series" [Washington: Catholic University of America Press, 1953]), p. 2.
2. Piper, *op. cit.,* p. 179.
3. Those interested can find a detailed discussion of this topic in Francis J. Connell, *Morals in Politics and Professions* (Westminster, Md.: Newman Press, 1946). See particularly his chapter on "The Catholic Lawyer." Also see John Denis Davis, *The Moral Obligations of Catholic Civil Judges* (Washington: Catholic University Press, 1954), particularly his chapter on "The Catholic Church and Divorce Cases."
4. State *ex rel.* Baker vs. Bird, 253 Mo. 569, 162 S.W. 149 (1913).

5. Purinton vs. Jamrock, 195 Mass. 187, 199-200; 80 N.E. 802, 805.

6. 29 *Harvard Law Review* 497 (1915-16).

7. Leo Pfeffer, "Religion in the Upbringing of Children," *Boston University Law Review*, June, 1955, p. 353.

8. *Ibid.*, p. 336.

9. For an account of this decision, see *Pittsburgh Press*, March 14, 1961.

10. Purinton vs. Jamrock, *op. cit.*

11. *In re Laura Doyle*, 16 Mo. App. 159 (1884).

12. *Re Gally*, 328 Mass. (1952).

13. *Ibid.*

14. See the Boston *Pilot*, June 8, and July 5, 1952.

15. Martin vs. Martin, 308 N. Y. 136, 123, N.E. 2d 813 (1954).

16. Pfeffer, "Religion in the Upbringing of Children," *op. cit.*, p. 361.

17. Brewer vs. Cary, Supre 148 Missouri Appeals, 193/127 S.W. 685 (1920).

18. Denton vs. James, 107 Kan. 729, 193 Pac. 307, 12 Al. R. 1146.

19. *In re Butcher's Estate*, 266 Pa. 479, 109, Atl. 683.

20. Lynch vs. Uhlenhopp, 248 Iowa Reports, 48862 (1956-67).

21. Diemer vs. Diemer, *op. cit.*

22. See also Magoun vs. Illinois Trust and Savings Bank, 170 U. S. 282, 288 (1898), and People *ex rel*, Portnoy vs. Strasser, 303 N. Y. 539, 104, N.E. 2d 895 (1925).

23. For a discussion of this point see "Enforceability of Ante-nuptial Contracts of Mixed Marriages," 50 *Yale Law Journal*, May, 1941, p. 1289.

24. Begley vs. Begley, *Now York Law Journal*, June 6, 1961, and June 14, 1960.

25. *Re Santos*, 278 App. Div. N. Y. 373 (1951). The case is discussed in Leo Pfeffer, *Church, State, and Freedom* (Boston: The Beacon Press, 1953), pp. 588 ff.

26. *Ibid.*, p. 590.

27. Ramon vs. Ramon, 34 N.Y.S.2d, 100.

28. Weinberger vs. Van Hessen, 220 N.Y. 294, 183 N.E. 429, 430.

29. Pfeffer, *Church, State, and Freedom,* pp. 360-61.

30. Martin vs. Martin, *op. cit.*

Bibliography

Marriage Counseling: a Case Book. New York: Association Press, 1958.

AYRINHAC, H. A. *Marriage Legislation in the New Code of Canon Law.* New York: Benziger, 1919.

BAILEY, D. S. *The Mystery of Love and Marriage: A Study in the Theology of Sex Relations.* New York: Harper & Brothers, 1952.

BAINTON, ROLAND H. *What Christianity Says About Sex, Love, and Marriage.* New York: Association Press, 1957.

BARRON, MILTON L. *People Who Intermarry; Intermarriage in a New England Industrial Community.* Syracuse: University Press, 1947.

BLACK, ALGERNON DAVID. *If I Marry Outside My Religion.* New York: Public Affairs Committee, 1954.

BLANSHARD, PAUL. *American Freedom and Catholic Power.* Boston: Beacon Press, 1958.

BOSSARD, JAMES H. S. *One Marriage, Two Faiths.* New York: Ronald Press, 1957.

BOUSCAREN, T. LINCOLN, and ELLIS, ADAM C. *Canon Law; a Text and Commentary.* Milwaukee: Bruce, 1951, 1957.

BOUSCAREN, T. LINCOLN. *Canon Law Digest: Officially Published Documents Affecting the Code of Canon Law.* Milwaukee: Bruce, 1934, 1943, 1954.

BOWMAN, HENRY A. *A Christian Interpretation of Marriage.* Philadelphia: The Westminster Press, 1959.

CLEMENS, A. H. *Marriage Education and Counseling.* Washington, D.C.: Catholic University Press, 1951.

COLACCI, MARIO. *Christian Marriage Today*. Minneapolis: Augsburg Press, 1958.

CONNELL, FRANCIS J. *Morals in Politics and Professions: A Guide for Catholics in Public Life*. Westminster, Md.: Newman Press, 1955.

DAVIS, JOHN DENNIS. *The Moral Obligations of Catholic Civil Judges*. Washington, D.C., Catholic University Press, 1954.

DOHENY, WILLIAM J. *Canonical Procedures in Matrimonial Cases*. Milwaukee: Bruce, 1948.

FAGLEY, RICHARD M. *The Population Explosion and Christian Responsibility*. New York: Oxford University Press, 1960.

Ideals on Marriage and the Home. New York: Commission on the Church and Social Service, 1929.

GARRISON, WINFRED E. *Catholicism and the American Mind*. Chicago: Willett Clark & Co., 1928.

————. *A Protestant Manifesto*. New York: Abingdon Press, 1952.

HEALY, EDWIN F. *Medical Ethics*. Chicago: Loyola University Press, 1956.

HERBERMANN, CHARLES G. *et al* (ed.). *The Catholic Encyclopedia*. 15 vols. New York: Robert Appleton Co., 1907.

HILTNER, SEWARD. *Sex and the Christian Life*. New York: Association Press, 1957.

JONES, HERIBERT (ed.). *Moral Theology*. Westminster, Md.: Newman Press, 1957.

JONES, ILION T. *A Protestant Speaks His Mind*. Philadelphia: Westminster Press, n.d.

JOYCE, GEORGE H. *Christian Marriage*. New York: Sheed & Ward, 1933.

KELLY, GEORGE A. *The Catholic Marriage Manual*. New York: Random House, 1958.

LACEY, THOMAS A. *Marriage in Church and State*. London: R. C. Mortimer, 1947.

LEACH, WILLIAM H. *The Cokesbury Marriage Manual*. New York: Abingdon Press, 1958.

LORD, DANIEL A. *Questions I'm Asked About Marriage*. St. Louis: Queen's Work Press, 1938.

MACMILLAN, ARTHUR T. *Marriage, Divorce and the Church: Chaos or Reform—Which?* London: Society for Promoting Christian Knowledge, 1946.

_____. *What Is Christian Marriage?* London: Macmillan Co., 1944.

MCAULEY, CLAIRE. *What God Hath Not Joined.* New York: Sheed & Ward, 1961.

MAGUOAN, F. ALEXANDER. *Love and Marriage.* New York: Harper & Brothers, 1948.

MAIER, WALTER. *For Better, Not for Worse: A Manual of Christian Matrimony.* St. Louis: Concordia Publishing House, 1939.

MARX, ADOLPH. *The Declaration of Nullity of Marriages Contracted Outside the Church.* Washington, D.C.: Catholic University Press, 1943.

MUDD, EMILY H. *The Practice of Marriage Counseling.* New York: Association Press, 1951.

NASH, ARNOLD S. (ed.). *Education for Christian Marriage; Its Theory and Practice.* London: Macmillan Co., 1939.

National Catholic Almanac. Patterson, N.J.: St. Anthony's Guild, 1960.

NICHOLS, JAMES H. *History of Christianity.* New York: Ronald Press, 1956.

_____. *Primer for Protestants.* New York: Association Press, 1947.

NIEBUHR, REINHOLD. *The Children of Light and the Children of Darkness.* New York: Charles Scribner's Sons, 1944.

_____. *Interpretation of Christian Ethics.* New York: Meridian Books, 1956.

O'BRIEN, JOHN A. *The Truth About Mixed Marriages.* Huntington, Ind.: Our Sunday Visitor Press, 1953.

O'BRIEN, JOSEPH P. *The Right of the State to Make Disease an Impediment to Marriage.* Washington, D.C.: Catholic University Press, 1952.

PFEFFER, LEO. *Church, State and Freedom.* Boston: Beacon Press, 1953.

_____. *Religion in the Upbringing of Children.* Reprint. Boston: University Law Review, XXXV (June 1955).

PIKE, JAMES A. *If You Marry Outside Your Faith.* New York: Harper & Brothers, 1954.

PIPER, OTTO A. *The Biblical View of Sex and Marriage.* New York: Charles Scribner's Sons, 1960.

RYAN, JOHN A., and BOLAND, FRANCIS J. *Catholic Principles of Politics.* New York: Macmillan Co., 1958.

RYCROFT, W. STANLEY. *Religion and Faith in Latin America.* Philadelphia: Westminster Press, n.d.

SCHAFF, DAVID S. *Our Father's Faith and Ours: A Comparison Between Protestantism and Romanism.* New York: G. P. Putnam, 1928.

SCHNEPP, G. J. *Leakage from a Catholic Parish.* Washington, D. C.: Catholic University Press, 1942.

SHENK, F. L. *Mixed Religion and Disparity of Cult.* Washington, D. C.: Catholic University Press, 1929.

STOKES, ANSON PHELPS. *Church and State in the United States.* 3 vols. New York: Harper & Brothers, 1950.

SULLOWAY, ALVAH W. *Birth Control and Catholic Doctrine.* Boston: Beacon Press, 1959.

TORPEY, WILLIAM G. *Judicial Doctrines of Religious Rights in America.* Chapel Hill, N. C.: University of North Carolina Press, 1948.

VINCENT, CLARK E. *Readings in Marriage Counseling.* New York: Thomas Y. Crowell, 1957.

WESTBERG, GRANGER. *Premarital Counseling.* National Council of Churches, 1958.

WOODLOCK, THOMAS F. *The Catholic Pattern.* New York: Simon and Schuster, 1942.

WOYWOD, STANISLAUS, and SMITH, CALLISTUS. *A Practical Commentary on the Code of Canon Law.* 2 vols. London: B. Herder, 1948.

Index